10

MINUTE GUIDE TO

PERSONAL FINANCE FOR NEWLYWEDS

by Stewart H. Welch III

alpha books

Macmillan Spectrum/Alpha

A Division of Macmillan General Reference
A Simon & Schuster Macmillan Company
1633 Broadway, New York, NY 10019-6785

International Standard Book Number: 0-02-861118-7
Library of Congress Catalog Card Number: 96-068555

98 97 96   8 7 6 5 4 3 2 1

Interpretation of the printing code: the rightmost double-digit number is the year of the book's first printing; the rightmost single-digit number is the number of the book's printing. For example, a printing code of 96-1 shows that this copy of the book was printed during the first printing of the book in 1996.

Printed in the United States of America

Note: Reasonable care has been taken in the preparation of the text to ensure its clarity and accuracy. This book is sold with the understanding that the author and the publisher are not engaged in rendering legal, accounting, or other professional service. Laws vary from state to state, and readers with specific financial questions should seek the services of a professional advisor.

Publisher: Theresa Murtha

Development Editor: Debra Wishik Englander

Production Editor: Michael Thomas

Copy Editor: Lynn Northrup

Cover Designer: Dan Armstrong

Designer: Kim Scott

Indexer: Debra Myers

Production Team: Heather Butler, Angela Calvert, Dan Caparo, Jason Hand, Clint Lahnen, Bobbi Satterfield, Karen Walsh

CONTENTS

INTRODUCTION

The commitment of marriage brings forth excitement and new challenges. The purpose of this book is to help you meet the challenge of building a successful financial future.

Unlike other skills that you may have learned at school, you may be ill-equipped to handle the many financial decisions you will face in the future. You may be confused or nervous about managing your money.

While this book is specifically written to help newlyweds, many of the principles and guidelines are appropriate for everyone.

As a soon-to-be-married, you will learn tips on dramatically reducing wedding costs. If you're a newlywed, you'll learn how to establish a budget and how to split expenses. Most important, you'll learn how to work together to set and achieve common financial goals.

This guide provides useful information on several important financial concerns. Much of your money goes to pay insurance premiums for life, health, auto, and homeowners coverage. You'll learn how to quickly evaluate your policies and get the best deals and the right coverage. As a couple, you will also face major financial decisions such as buying a home or starting a family. You will learn strategies that will enable you to meet these challenges as well. You'll also learn ways to reduce your taxes.

How to Get the Most from This Book

To gain the most from this book, begin with Lesson 1 and work your way through the last lesson. You'll find simple-to-use exercises that will help you build a sound financial game plan. For example, Lesson 15 offers an exercise on helping you set up and manage your own investment program.

You can also use this book as a quick reference guide for just about any financial decision you must make. For example, if you're uncertain how much life insurance you need, turn to Lesson 8.

In fact, each lesson is set up to allow you to cover one subject in about 10 minutes or so.

Conventions Used in This Book

To help you move through the lessons easily, the *10 Minute Guide to Personal Finance for Newlyweds* uses the following icons to alert you to important concepts:

 Plain English   New or unfamiliar terms are defined in "plain English."

 Tip   These are ideas that will help you avoid confusion.

Panic Button   This icon is used to highlight common problems that you may face.

What to Do Now

You should get a pen and pad and look at the Contents to get a sense of the order of the book. Then, open to Lesson 1 to begin the process of building your financial future. The *10 Minute Guide to Personal Finance for Newlyweds* puts you in charge of your financial life!

Acknowledgements

The completion of this book would not have been possible without the technical and moral support of many people.

My heartfelt thanks go out to Debra Wishik Englander, my editor and a dear friend since 1987. Debby has had a profound impact on my career and I will forever be indebted to her. Without her encouragement and assistance this book would not have been possible.

Lynn Northrup and Michael Thomas assisted with the editing and showed a knack for details and organizational skills that always impressed me. I also want to thank Theresa Murtha, my publisher, and Simon and Schuster Macmillan Company for giving me the opportunity to work on this project.

All of my associates at THE WELCH GROUP not only tolerated but were supportive of the many hours I spent on this project. A special thanks to Christina Payne, Sheri Robinson, CPA, Chad McWhirter, and Isabel Corley. Christina in particular, spent many long hours working with me to ensure the quality of this material.

For technical advice, I owe a debt of gratitude to Leon Ashford, Kelly Byrne, Bob Holman, CPA, Mike Priestley, Al Reynolds, and Mark Wesson. While we did not always agree on every issue, each of them displayed a high degree of knowledge, integrity, and professionalism.

The many wonderful clients who I have worked with over the years are due credit as well. My mission of meeting their needs always inspires me to continue to learn and grow both professionally and personally.

Finally, I owe a particular note of thanks to my family. From my parents and my sisters, I've received a lifetime of moral support. My wife and best friend, Kathie, always provides encouragement, a hug, and a smile just when I need it.

BEFORE THE
I Do's

In this lesson, you learn the importance of sharing personal financial information, goals, and money fears with your future marriage partner. You also learn how to budget for your wedding, especially if you're looking to cut your expenses.

SHARING FINANCIAL INFORMATION: WHERE DO YOU START?

Sharing personal financial information is an important building block for your marriage. If either of you has money problems, you can identify them early on and begin solving them together.

WHAT YOU OWN, WHAT YOU OWE

Begin sharing financial information by making a list of your assets and liabilities. Use Table 1.1 to assist you.

Table 1.1

Assets (what you own)
1. Value of bank, savings, money market accounts $_____
2. Personal investments: stocks, bonds, mutual funds $_____
3. Retirement plan values: IRAs, vested interest in
    company retirement plan $_____
4. Market value of real estate: residence, land, etc. $_____
5. Personal property: cars, furniture, jewelry, etc. $_____
6. Other assets. Anything not previously covered
    (i.e., ownership in a business) $_____

Total $_____

Liabilities
1. Amount you owe on credit cards and charge cards $_____
2. Personal loans. How much you owe individuals $_____
3. Auto loans. How much you owe on car loans $_____
4. Mortgage loans. How much you owe on a house
    or other real estate $_____
5. Other liabilities. Any financial obligation not
    previously covered (i.e., Unpaid income taxes, etc.) $_____

Total $_____

Your income
1. Salary. Your total pay annually $_____
2. Other income. Any other income you receive (annually) $_____

Total $_____

Assets   Your *assets* are everything that you own, such as money in the bank, automobiles, investments, and real estate.

Liabilities   Your *liabilities* are everything that you owe, such as credit card balances, car notes, and home mortgages.

WHAT YOU MAKE

To start the budget process, you and your fiancé need to share information about your incomes. The bottom section of Table 1.1 provides space for this.

By sharing this information now, you will eliminate any potential post-wedding surprises. Finding out that your spouse has serious financial problems is not the right way to start off your marriage.

Once you have shared your basic financial information, you can complete the following exercises.

ESTABLISH YOUR FINANCIAL GOALS

Make a list of both short-term and intermediate-term financial objectives you want to work on. Short-term objectives are those that are attainable within a year's time. Long-term objectives take from one to five years to achieve. Short-term objectives include paying wedding expenses, saving for a honeymoon trip, building up a savings cushion, or saving for some new furnishings. Long-term objectives include saving for the down payment on a home or saving to pay cash for a new car.

You and your fiancé should complete this exercise separately. After both of you have finished, you should get together to develop common priorities. It's essential that both of you have input on the broad decisions. You will learn more about details in the next lesson. For now, decide on the broad goals the two of you will strive to achieve.

DISCUSS YOUR WORST (FINANCIAL) NIGHTMARE

In this exercise, you and your fiancé should have an open discussion regarding your feelings about money. What are your concerns? If you identify problems, discuss possible solutions. For example, if you discover that neither of you has much experience in dealing with money matters, you can take a financial planning course together or work together using a book such as this one.

It may be hard for you to have an honest discussion about your finances. However, it's important to create a trusting relationship so you'll be able to talk about money in both good and bad times. Begin now and you will reap the benefits for many years to come.

YOUR WEDDING: CONTROLLING THE COSTS

A wedding is one of those major events that tends to take on a life of its own. Before you realize what has happened, you have spent far more money than you planned or can afford. To avoid this problem, you should establish a wedding budget and stick to it. Traditionally, parents of the bride and groom contribute toward wedding expenses. If this is the case for your wedding, be sure to involve your parents in the budgeting process. Today, however, it is not unusual for the bride and groom to pay most, if not all, of the wedding cost.

Before you review the details of the budget, you should determine what you can afford to spend on the entire event. Table 1.2 lists some suggested percentages to use as guidelines for expenses.

Table 1.2	Total wedding budget $_____	
Stationery items (3%)	estimated cost $_____	actual cost $_____
Bridal attire (10%)	estimated cost $_____	actual cost $_____
Reception (40%)	estimated cost $_____	actual cost $_____
Flowers (8%)	estimated cost $_____	actual cost $_____
Music (3%)	estimated cost $_____	actual cost $_____
Photographs (7%)	estimated cost $_____	actual cost $_____
Gifts-attendants (2%)	estimated cost $_____	actual cost $_____
Honeymoon (20%)	estimated cost $_____	actual cost $_____
Misc. (i.e., special parties) (7%)	estimated cost $_____	actual cost $_____
	Total estimated cost $_____	Total actual cost $_____

Obviously, as you customize your own wedding, these guidelines will vary. To help keep track of these expenses, put all receipts and contracts pertaining to your wedding in a large envelope.

Tips for Cutting Wedding Costs

Naturally, you want your wedding to be memorable, but you don't have to go broke. Here are some cost-cutting strategies:

- *Flowers.* If another wedding is scheduled at your church on the day yours is planned, consider sharing the flowers for the ceremony with the other couple. Or rent silk flowers.

- *Wedding dress.* Instead of buying an expensive new wedding dress, consider borrowing, renting, or buying a dress from a consignment shop.

- *Headpiece.* Make your headpiece yourself. It's easy and will save you a lot of money. Or borrow one.

- *Photography.* Decide in advance, with your photographer, exactly what pictures you want. Have your friends and family bring cameras as well so you'll have many impromptu shots. Or put inexpensive disposable cameras on each table.

- *Food.* If you're serving a meal, shop around. Prices vary according to the supplier, type of food, and time of day. Some caterers will allow you to sample their work. Even if you can't taste the food in advance, any good caterer should provide you with references. If you're on a tight budget, consider having an early-morning wedding and serving only light refreshments.

- *Facility.* Consider holding the wedding and/or the reception at someone's home. Renting a nice tent can be much less expensive than renting a commercial facility. Also, if you belong to a church or synagogue, you may be able to use its facilities at a nominal cost.

- *Guests.* Limit your guest list. Caterers often charge by the head. Diplomatically, encourage your families not to invite long-lost cousins or neighbors you haven't seen in years.

- *Honeymoon.* When planning your honeymoon, remember that it is always off-season somewhere. Off-season is synonymous with lower rates. For example, a week in Breckenridge, Colorado during the summer costs less than half what it would cost if you went during ski season. Although you can't ski, you can enjoy tennis, golf, hiking, horseback riding, and breathtaking scenery. Locals insist this is the best time of year.

  Also, consider staying at a bed-and-breakfast rather than a large hotel. Many B&Bs are quite elegant and romantic, and they often cost significantly less than hotels.

- *Invitations.* Learn calligraphy and address your invitations yourself rather than hiring someone. You can also reduce the cost of the invitations by using thermography instead of engraving.

In this lesson, you learned how open communication about your finances and your attitudes about money can help create a solid foundation for your marriage. You also learned how to budget for your wedding. In the next lesson, you learn how to develop your own personal financial plan based on your goals and priorities.

2

SECOND HONEYMOON: THE FINANCIAL SUMMIT WEEKEND

In this lesson, you learn the steps in the financial planning process, including figuring out your net worth and how to begin developing your financial goals.

PLANNING: THE KEY TO FINANCIAL SUCCESS

After your honeymoon, you should begin planning your financial future. Studies indicate that 95 percent of all Americans never achieve financial independence, primarily because they don't develop a *written* financial plan. If you are going to build a strong financial future, your plans must have time to work. If you start planning now, you'll be amazed at the results in ten years. In fact, you can achieve total financial independence within twenty years by developing and following a sound financial plan.

Financial Independence   Financial independence means your investments produce enough income to meet your lifestyle needs for the rest of your life. For example, if you and your spouse's combined income is $50,000 per year, you would be financially independent if your investments produced $50,000 per year, adjusted for inflation, for the rest of your lives.

YOUR FINANCIAL PLAN

The following is an overview of the steps in the financial planning process.

- *Step 1.* Answer the question "Where am I now?" by determining your net worth.

Net Worth   Your net worth is the difference between everything you own and everything you owe.

- *Step 2.* Answer the question "Where am I going?" by spelling out your specific financial goals and priorities.

- *Step 3.* Answer the question "How am I going to get there?" This involves managing your income, expenses, and investments, otherwise known as budgeting.

- *Step 4.* Implement your plan. The best plan in the world is meaningless if you don't implement it.

- *Step 5.* Review your plan periodically. You will need to make adjustments in order to stay on your financial course.

You will need time and concentrated effort to develop your financial plan. As a couple, you should set aside a weekend for a "financial summit."

To prepare for your financial summit, you'll need to gather certain information:

- *Bank account balances.* Check with your bank if you don't know your balance.

- *Investment account values.* If you own stocks, bonds, mutual funds, CDs, money market accounts, or savings accounts, you'll need to determine the values.

- *Pay stubs.* Gather your four most recent pay stubs.

- *Retirement plan statements.* If you have money in IRA accounts or company retirement plans, you'll need to know your balances as well as who is named as the beneficiary of your retirement plans.

 Often newlyweds forget to change the beneficiary designation of their retirement plan to their new spouse.

- *Life insurance.* Contact your agent or company employee benefits department (for group life insurance) and get information on the amounts of insurance, current beneficiary, premiums, surrender values, and loans.

- *Disability income.* If you own individual disability income insurance, find your policy. Also, check with your employer to see if it offers group disability income insurance. Find out the monthly benefit, when the benefit begins paying, and for how long the benefit is paid.

- *Property and casualty.* Gather your homeowners or renters and auto insurance policies.

- *Health insurance.* Have your policy or group health insurance summary available.

- *Wills.* If you have a will, have it available.

- *Employee Benefits Summary.* Get a summary of your benefits from your employer.

- *Notes and mortgages.* Contact your lenders to find out the total amount you owe on notes and mortgages. Also, make sure you know when the loans will be paid off, and the total of your monthly payments.

- *Credit cards and charge cards.* Get your most recent statements or call your credit card and charge card companies to find out your balance on each debt. Also, find out what your minimum required monthly payments are.

After you have gathered this basic financial data, you are ready to get started. By following the agenda on the next page, you should move smoothly through the financial planning process.

AGENDA FOR THE FINANCIAL SUMMIT WEEKEND

You should plan to set aside a few days to establish the framework of your financial plan. The following two-day format breaks the process into blocks of time. Work at your own pace—remember, everyone is different. You may find that you move quickly through some sections, whereas others take more time than is estimated.

DAY 1: Develop your net worth statement (2 hours)

Your net worth statement provides a "snapshot" of your financial picture at a particular point in time. It simply lists all of your assets (what you own) and all of your liabilities (what you owe). Detailed assistance in completing your net worth statement is found later in this lesson.

Define your goals (2 hours)

You will need to develop a list of both your short-term and long-term goals. For assistance in goal planning, see "Setting Goals and Priorities" later in this lesson.

Manage financial risks (4 hours)

Financial risks include all of the insurance decisions you will need to make. For life insurance, see Lessons 7 and 8. Auto insurance is explained in Lesson 9. Homeowners and personal property insurance are discussed in Lesson 10. For health and disability insurance, see Lesson 11. Personal liability insurance is outlined in Lesson 9.

DAY 2: Develop a budget (4 hours)

Your objective here is to develop a detailed spending plan for the next 12 months. See Lesson 3 for detailed assistance.

Investments and financial independence planning (3 hours)

You will need to develop an investment plan that is designed to achieve your long-term goal of financial independence. For help, see Lessons 14 and 15 on Investing.

It takes time to develop a personal financial plan. By developing one early in your marriage, you significantly increase your chances of becoming financially independent and you're also more likely to have a successful marriage. Remember, most failed marriages are caused in part by financial problems.

YOUR NET WORTH

The first thing you need to do is develop a net worth statement. Start by listing your assets in the following table.

PERSONAL FINANCIAL STATEMENT
FOR

_____

DATE _____

ASSETS

Cash & Cash Equivalents

1. Cash on Hand	$ _____
2. Cash in Checking Account	$ _____
3. Cash in Savings Account	$ _____
4. Life Insurance Cash Value	$ _____
5. Savings Bonds	$ _____
6. Accounts Receivable	$ _____
	Total $ _____

Personal Property (Estimated Current Market Value)

7. Household Furnishings	$ _____
8. Special Items (Car, Boat, Jewelry)	$ _____
9. Miscellaneous Property	$ _____
	Total $ _____

Real Estate (Estimated Current Market Value)

10. Residence(s)	$ _____
11. Other Properties	$ _____
	Total $ _____

Investments (Estimated Current Market Value)

12. Stocks	$ _____
13. Bonds	$ _____
14. Mutual Funds	$ _____
15. Vested Interest in a Pension Plan	$ _____
16. Keogh, IRA, or Tax Sheltered Annuity	$ _____
17. Equity Interest in a Business	$ _____
18. Other Investments	$ _____
	Total $ _____

TOTAL ASSETS $

Now add up all your individual asset values. The result is the value of your total assets. Hopefully, that's the good news. Now list your liabilities in the following "Liabilities" table.

LIABILITIES		
Current Liabilities		
1. Charge Account Balance	$ _____	
2. Credit Card Balance	$ _____	
	Total	$ _____
Amounts Owed on Loans		
3. Mortgage(s)	$ _____	
4. Automobile Loan(s)	$ _____	
5. Personal Loans	$ _____	
6. Installment Loans	$ _____	
7. Life Insurance Loans	$ _____	
	Total	$ _____
Misc Liabilities		
8. Unpaid Income Taxes	$ _____	
9. Other Liabilities	$ _____	
	Total	$ _____
TOTAL LIABILITIES	**$**	
NET WORTH	**$**	

Now add up all of your liabilities to determine your total liabilities. By subtracting your total liabilities from your total assets, you will arrive at your net worth. Your net worth tells you how much money you would have left if you sold everything you owned and paid off everything you owe. Don't be discouraged if your net worth is negligible or even negative. That's why you're developing a financial plan.

To complete your financial statement, complete the "Statement of Income" table. Add up all items of income to determine your total annual income.

```
┌─────────────────────────────────────┐
│                                     │
│   STATEMENT OF INCOME               │
│                                     │
│   1. Salary            $_____      │
│      Salary of Spouse  $_____      │
│   2. Bonuses           $_____      │
│   3. Interest          $_____      │
│   4. Dividends         $_____      │
│   5. Other Income      $_____      │
│                                     │
│   TOTAL INCOME $                    │
│                                     │
└─────────────────────────────────────┘
```

In order to measure your financial progress, you will need to update your net worth statement at least once a year. Be sure to save all your statements. You will want to compare your progress from year to year.

SETTING GOALS AND PRIORITIES

If the net worth statement tells you where you are, the goals statement tells you where you are going.

When you write a goal, it should be one that both of you share and something that you want badly enough to work for. Ideally, it should be realistic and specific, so that you can measure your results.

Develop a list of both short-term and long-term goals. Next, prioritize your goals. If you could accomplish only one of your goals, which would you choose? Having accomplished that goal, which would be next? Continue this process until you have prioritized all the goals on your lists. This exercise should be done separately by each spouse. Then compare your notes and compile a common list of your goals, listing your highest-priority goal first.

Now focus on your number-one goal. What do you need to begin doing now in order to move toward accomplishing this goal? How much do you need to save each month? What is the most appropriate investment vehicle? Develop a written plan of action that you believe will best accomplish this goal in the shortest period of time. Once it is completed, move to your next goal. Continue this process until you have a written plan for all your goals.

Here's an example. Your number-one goal is to buy a home in the next 24 months. You decide you can afford to spend $150,000. You need to save $20,000—$15,000 for the down payment and $5,000 for closing costs. The remaining $130,000 will be financed with payments of approximately $1,300 per month (see Lesson 5 for guidelines). Because you have $5,000 already in savings, you'll need to save approximately $625 per month for 24 months to make up the difference. You decide the best way to do this is through automatic payroll deductions to your credit union.

Developing precise goals is not a simple task. This will, in effect, be your "first draft." You will probably have to make revisions as you work your goals into your budget. Also, it's likely that you won't have the financial resources to begin working on all of your goals at once. This is why you have prioritized them. Over time, you can accomplish all of your goals if you develop a detailed written plan, stick to it, and make adjustments along the way.

In this lesson, you learned the importance of planning in order to achieve financial success. In the next lesson, you learn how to set up a realistic budget and learn strategies to cut your expenses without sacrificing your lifestyle.

Budgeting: Getting the Most from Your Earnings

In this lesson, you learn how to set your budget so you can gain control of your income and expenses and learn how to save more money.

The Budgeting Process

To achieve financial independence, you must spend less than you make. This means you need to carefully control your expenses. Three guiding principles will help keep you on track:

- Establish a budget that preallocates your income.

- Stop spending when your spending limit is reached.

- Monitor where you are in relation to your spending plan.

Developing your budget involves four steps:

- *Step 1.* Determine what you have spent in the past.
  You will need to review the past twelve months' expenditures. Look at your canceled checks and credit
  card statements. Using Form 3.1 as a guide, divide
  your expenses into appropriate categories. Whereas
  many expenses recur monthly, others will be
  irregular.

- *Step 2.* Determine what you can do to trim expenses.
  The money you save on expenses can be used for
  savings and investments. See "Strategies for Saving
  Money and Getting Ahead" later in this lesson.

- *Step 3.* Establish your budget. Now that you have
  reviewed past spending patterns and expense reduction strategies, you are ready to set up your budget.
  Use one Form 3.1 for each of the next twelve
  months. Don't forget to enter irregular expenses in
  the month they come due.

- *Step 4.* Monitor your budget. At the end of each
  month, you need to compare your actual expenses to
  your budgeted expenses. You will probably have to
  make some adjustments to your budget, but remember that your expenses cannot exceed your income.

Don't be discouraged if your initial budgeting efforts seem
futile. It takes most people one to two years to become profi-
cient budgeters. In the long run, you will develop a sixth sense
when it comes to managing expenses.

Form 3-1

BUDGET WORKSHEET
FOR MONTH OF

	BUDGET AMOUNT	ACTUAL AMOUNT	DIFFERENCE
GROSS INCOME			
Less: Giving (10%)			
Taxes (17%)			
Investment/Savings (10%)			
Housing (25%)			
Food (10%)			
Clothing (4%)			
Transportation (5%)			
Entertain./Recreation (5%)			
Medical (2%)			
Insurance (4%)			
Children (3%)			
Gifts (2%)			
Miscellaneous (3%)			
TOTAL LIVING EXPENSES (90%)			

ASSUMPTIONS:
1. Guideline percentages based on $40,000 gross income
2. Medical insurance is largely paid by employer
3. Tax deductions are religious and charitable giving, home mortgage interest, state and property taxes
4. Cash flow margin can be used for other expenses: (debt, education, savings, retirement, etc.)

WHO PAYS FOR WHAT?

Your expenses should be divided between you and your spouse. Review the budget together and divide up the expenses based on who usually pays each kind of bill. For instance, if one of you does most of the grocery shopping, that person should be responsible for groceries.

To minimize confusion, you should use two checking accounts. Both accounts can be joint checking accounts. After you decide who is responsible for paying each bill, you may have to transfer some income from one spouse's account to the other. This "shifting" is part of the budgeting process.

Two people spending out of one checkbook does not work unless one person is paying all of the bills and the other person is receiving a weekly "allowance" for out-of-pocket expenses. With two people writing checks, it is difficult to keep track of how much money is in the account at all times.

KEEPING RECORDS

Most companies allow you a 15- to 30-day grace period in which to pay bills. During this time, no interest or penalties accrue. To simplify the bill-paying process, place bills in a large folder as they come in. Then, twice a month, around the 15th and 30th, set aside a time to pay all accumulated bills. At the end of the month, transfer your receipts and bank statements to a large envelope marked with the current month. For example, January bills go in your January envelope. This will help you keep your records straight. If you enjoy working on a computer, you may want to use Quicken software to pay your bills and help you with your budget. This software can be purchased at any computer store.

As you pay and record your expenses, identify and segregate those that may be tax deductible. This will be a real time saver at income tax time.

STRATEGIES FOR SAVING MONEY AND GETTING AHEAD

Maintaining control over income and expenses can be a formidable task. Most people have a tendency to spend with very little thought. Once you begin to pay attention to all of your expenses, you will save thousands of dollars while sacrificing very little of your lifestyle. Here are some suggestions:

- Pay yourself first. Most people's savings plan consists of saving whatever is left over at the end of the month. Unfortunately, there's rarely any money left over. By paying yourself first, you guarantee that you are headed down the path to financial independence.

 tip To assure that you pay yourself first, set up an automatic deduction from each paycheck. This can either be done by your employer making a direct deposit to your credit union or by your bank automatically depositing to your savings account.

- Don't loan the government money. You may have your employer over-withhold taxes from your paycheck so that you get a refund at tax time. This amounts to a tax-free loan to the government. Instead, have your employer withhold an adequate amount to cover your liability and set up an automatic savings program. That way your money is working for your benefit, not the government's.

If you are self-employed, set aside an appropriate amount of money to cover taxes. Put this money into a savings account. Don't wait until your quarterly taxes are due—you'll find yourself behind and playing catch-up the rest of the year.

- Build emergency reserves. Financial surprises occur with amazing regularity. To be prepared, you need an emergency reserve account equal to three to six months income. To build up this account, have 2–5 percent of your paycheck automatically deposited into a savings account.

- Review your mortgage interest rate. Compare current mortgage rates to your mortgage rate. If the current rates are 1 1/2 to 2 percent lower, you should consider refinancing.

- Save on utilities. When you add up all the money you spend on utilities, you'll see that it is a big portion of your budget. Conservation is the best way to cut expenses here.

In summer months, use a ceiling fan to save money by reducing the use of air conditioning. Likewise, in the winter months, wear warm clothes around the house to reduce the use of your furnace.

Consider adding insulation in your attic. Proper insulation can cut heating and cooling bills by 10 percent or more.

See if your utility company provides an "energy efficiency survey." This survey can tell you if you have energy leaks in your home and how to eliminate them.

Reduce long-distance telephone charges by making your calls in the evening and on weekends as much as possible. This alone can cut your long-distance charges as much as 50 percent. Also, shop long-distance carriers. A little bit of homework can save you a lot of money. Consider writing instead of calling.

Use water-saving devices for your showers and toilets, and turn down your water heater during the summer months.

• Save on your grocery bill. Depending on your income, food costs can easily represent 10 percent or more of your budget. A little bit of thought and planning can go a long way toward cutting expenses.

Join a nearby warehouse club. Prices are cheaper on most items. See if you can shop with friends or other family members because you usually have to buy items in large quantities.

 When shopping at wholesale clubs, don't buy more perishables than you will consume, and be careful not to buy things you don't need just because they're a great deal.

Avoid buying junk food as much as possible. Soft drinks, chips, and candy are not only bad for you, but are very expensive compared to most staple goods.

Plan meals. Plan one or two weeks' worth of meals before you go to the grocery store. Make a list of the items you will need and stick to it when you're there. This will save time and help you avoid making unplanned and unnecessary purchases.

Use coupons. Although clipping coupons is not for everyone, coupons can save you money if you use them correctly. Use them only for items and brands that you normally use.

Buy store brands instead of national brands. This can cut your costs by 30 percent or more per item. Many store brands are the same quality as the national brands. The only difference is that the store brand does not advertise and that savings is passed on to you.

- Limit your dining out. Eating at a restaurant is fun, but it can be expensive. It should definitely be considered a luxury. When you do eat out, lower your bill by avoiding alcohol, appetizers, and desserts. Many restaurant portions are large. Don't be embarrassed to split a dinner with your spouse. Not only will you save money, you'll avoid overeating. Likewise, have your waiter "doggie bag" your leftovers. By doing so, you've saved the cost of one more meal.

- Save on household goods and appliances. When buying household goods such as detergent and paper products, shop wholesale rather than retail. Wholesale clubs use massive buying strategies and low overhead facilities in order to pass savings on to you. When buying household appliances such as a washer and dryer, look for bargains at "scratch-and-dent" sales, garage sales, or in the classified section of the newspaper.

- Plan clothing purchases. To save money on clothing, plan ahead and take advantage of seasonal sales. Consider shopping at consignment shops, especially for children's clothing. Other bargains can be found at discount department stores and outlet malls. Again, buy only what you need, not what is a great deal.

- Maintain your automobile. The best car deal is investing in the maintenance of your current car. When you decide to buy a new car, consider a used one that is 24–36 months old. A car's value decreases the most during this period of time.

tip
Fuel and insurance are major expenses of owning an automobile. Consider these expenses before buying your next car. Also, shop around when you need your car repaired, because prices and quality of repair work vary widely.

- Ask for generic prescriptive drugs and medicines. You'll often save up to 50 percent by using generic-brand prescriptions.

Generic   Generic brands are medicines with virtually the same ingredients as used in the more expensive brand-name medicines.

- Vacation during the off-season. You can travel to first-class resorts at big discounts if you go during the off-season.

- Remember, it's the thought that counts. If you added up how much money you spend each year on gifts, you'd be amazed. A homemade pound cake or hand-written note mean as much, if not more, than an expensive gift.

- Negotiate rent increases. Landlords enjoy having good tenants. It's in a landlord's best interest to keep current tenants rather than find new ones. When a new tenant moves in, the landlord must spend money painting and cleaning the apartment. Assuming you are a good tenant, use your status to negotiate your rent increases. If your landlord is uncooperative, look for less expensive property to rent.

Making a budget work requires a certain mindset that focuses on all expenses. You have to decide which luxuries are important and which are not. Remember, everyone deserves a few indulgences. The key is not wasting money on things that aren't important to you.

In this lesson, you learned how to set up your budget and how to cut expenses. In the next lesson, you will begin to learn how to control debt.

4

UNDERSTANDING AND CONTROLLING DEBT

In this lesson, you learn how to manage debt. You also learn what causes debt problems and how you can solve these problems.

THE DEBT RULE

Too much debt will make it very difficult for you to achieve financial independence. Although it's impractical to avoid debt completely, you should be able to maintain appropriate control of your debt.

You should strive to avoid debt as much as possible. However, the key Debt Rule is that if you must borrow to buy something, the *economic value* of what you're borrowing money to buy must always exceed the indebtedness. That way, if you get into financial trouble, you can sell the item and raise enough money to pay off your loan. Some items, such as clothing, have very little value after they're purchased and should not be bought using borrowed money. Other items, such as automobiles, depreciate rapidly and therefore require that you save for a larger down payment in order to stay within the guidelines of the Debt Rule.

Depreciation   A depreciating asset is something you own that goes down in value over time. For example, most cars are worth less every month you own them.

If you've already broken the Debt Rule, you can still do something about it. First, you need to understand the causes of debt problems.

CURING DEBT PROBLEMS

Debt problems are caused by different factors. The following section explains some of the most common problems and their solutions. If you find your problems are different, take a piece of paper and try to come up with your own solutions.

DEBT PROBLEM #1: CREDIT CARDS

It's easy to get credit. You probably receive credit card offers through the mail often. Credit card companies know that when you have credit cards you're likely to spend more. Unfortunately, when you spend more, you'll probably only make the minimum monthly payments. This is the credit card trap that you want to avoid. There are a few ways you can avoid this trap:

SOLUTION #1

Reduce the number of credit cards you have. You need only one or two. All retail stores will accept either a major credit card or a personal check, so having a retail store charge card is unnecessary. By reducing the number of credit cards you have, you automatically reduce the risk for misuse.

SOLUTION #2

Knowing how much you've charged on all your cards will help you keep track of your debts. To keep better records, enter charges directly into your checkbook just as you would if you had written a check. Subtract the charge from your balance. Why? You just spent the money so you must account for that expense immediately. Later, when you get your credit card statement, don't subtract the payment to your credit card company from your balance since you subtracted it earlier. See the following table for an example.

 tip By entering your credit card charges directly into your checkbook and subtracting the charge from your balance, you gain control over your credit card spending.

Date	Check number	To:	Amount of Deposit	Amount of Check	Balance
9/25	107	Power Company		$127.50	$1075.00
9/25	108	Gas Company		$ 25.00	$1050.00
9/27	**VISA**	**Best Department Store**		**$150.00**	**$ 900.00**
9/29	109	Best Grocery		$ 67.75	$ 832.25

DEBT PROBLEM #2: "KEEPING UP WITH THE JONESES" MENTALITY

Undoubtedly, you feel pressure to keep up with your peers. When your friends buy new sports cars, you think you should have one also. After all, if they can afford it, surely you can too. However, this attitude only leads to building a debt pyramid.

SOLUTION #1

Develop an attitude of contentment with your financial situation at this particular point in time. Before you make any purchase, ask yourself, "Is this something I need or something I want?" If it falls into the "want" category, try postponing the decision for a week or two. By giving yourself a cooling-off period, you're likely to find that logic will win over your emotional desires.

SOLUTION #2

Your neighbors who spend wildly likely have no long-term goals. You must focus on your long-term goals and resist excessive spending today.

DEBT PROBLEM #3: MONTHLY-PAYMENT MENTALITY

When you're considering purchasing a car, boat, furniture, or any other big-ticket items, you probably focus only on the size of your monthly payments. However, this view is a shortcut to financial disaster. You cannot become financially independent by frequent borrowing.

SOLUTION #1

If possible, postpone purchases until you have the cash to pay for them in full. This is called "delayed gratification." For example, you want to purchase a bedroom set that costs $6,000. The finance company offers you "no money down" with payments of $213 a month for 36 months. This brings the total cost to $7,668! It would be better if you delayed buying the set and instead began your savings plan. Then, when you have the cash, buy the set. Also, when you pay with cash, you are in a much better position to negotiate a lower price.

 tip The payment plans that many furniture companies offer include no money down and no interest payments. This "free" interest is built into the price of the furniture. If you are prepared to pay cash, you can often negotiate a savings of 10 to 20 percent.

Solution #2

If you have to borrow the money for a consumer purchase, follow the guidelines in Lesson 5.

Debt Problem #4: Failing to Plan for Major Events

You probably think about what you need only in terms of tomorrow or next week. This attitude inevitably leads to many financial surprises because you haven't considered home repairs, a new car, your child's wedding, your child's education, underpayment of income taxes, and so on.

Good planning requires you to look ahead one to five years to anticipate upcoming major expenses. For example, you know your car will eventually need to be replaced. If you ignore the inevitable, your only choice will be to borrow to meet your needs.

Solution

You should establish an emergency account equal to three to six months' salary for unexpected events such as major home repairs. You may need to set aside even more money for other expenditures, such as a new car or building an addition to your home. Start by putting aside between 2 and 5 percent of your take-home pay into a savings or money market account. Continue until this account reaches your target amount.

In this lesson, you learned why it's so easy to end up with too much debt and how you can avoid this problem. In the next lesson, you learn the true costs of debt as well as specific guidelines you can use when borrowing money.

5

GUIDELINES FOR BORROWING

In this lesson, you learn the true costs of debt and what debt guidelines you should follow in order to stay out of trouble.

TRUE COSTS OF DEBT

In order to achieve financial independence, you must get your money working for you. When you borrow money, your money is working for someone else—the bank—because you must repay the loan and also pay interest. The amount of interest you pay over the life of a loan can be enormous. For example, a $100,000 mortgage loan at 9 percent interest over 30 years requires a total payment of $289,664! Fortunately, your home will likely increase in value over time.

Consider two other examples: borrowing to buy a car and borrowing due to overspending.

BUYING A CAR

If you bought a car and borrowed $20,000 at 12.5 percent interest over a five-year term, the total cost of your loan would be $26,998. Your $6,998 of interest payments represent an increase in the total cost of the automobile of approximately 33 percent.

Assume you buy a car every five years. Over the next 40 years, you would buy eight cars at a total cost of $213,752, of which over $50,000 is interest. On the other hand, if you bought these cars without taking out a loan, you would be able to use the $50,000 you would have spent on interest in your investment program. If invested wisely, that $50,000 could grow to more than $750,000. This $750,000 is the true cost of borrowing.

OVERSPENDING

If you spend more than you make, you must borrow money to make ends meet. This borrowing often shows up in the form of increasing credit card debt. The following table shows you what overspending $1,000 per year over ten years really costs you.

To get out of debt over the next five years, you must first stop the $1,000 overspending per year. To repay principle and interest will cost an additional $3,000 a year, or approximately $333 per month. The total reduction in cash flow is $4,000 each year. Getting out of debt is much harder than getting into debt.

Year	Overspending	Debt Accumulation	Interest at 18%
1	$1,000	$1,000	$180
2	$1,000	$2,000	$360
3	$1,000	$3,000	$540
4	$1,000	$4,000	$720
5	$1,000	$5,000	$900
6	$1,000	$6,000	$1,080
7	$1,000	$7,000	$1,260
8	$1,000	$8,000	$1,440
9	$1,000	$9,000	$1,620
10	$1,000	$10,000	$1,800
Totals	$10,000		$9,900

Before borrowing money, ask yourself these five questions:

- *Does it make economic sense?* At a minimum, anything you borrow money to buy should be worth at least what you owe. That way, if you find you cannot make the payments, you can sell the item and pay off your loan. Never borrow money for intangible things like vacations.

- *Does my spouse agree with taking on this debt?* As discussed in Lesson 1, it's essential for couples to discuss financial issues openly. When you're considering taking on new debt, be certain you both agree it is the right thing for you to do.

- *Will borrowing this money result in achieving a personal goal that can't be met any other way?* Look for alternatives to borrowing. Could you raise cash through a garage sale? Do you have a boat or car that you could sell to raise cash? Could you wait 12–24 months while you saved the money to pay cash? Remember, debt always reduces your future lifestyle. Avoid it if you can.

- *Is what I'm borrowing money to buy going to satisfy a need or a greed?* A greed can be defined as something you want rather than need. Be careful about borrowing money to satisfy your wants. Because wants are unlimited, you'll never be able to borrow enough money to satisfy them.

- *Do I have a guaranteed way to repay this loan?* The best solution here is to be sure that what you buy has economic value. If not, make sure you have something of economic value that can guarantee the debt. For example, you borrow $5,000 to buy a bedroom set. Used furniture has little economic value, so you need a substitute. Say you have $5,000 in a Certificate of Deposit that you can earmark to cover this debt. Now you have a guaranteed way to repay the loan.

Specific Guidelines for Debt

If you must borrow money for purchases, stay within the following guidelines. These guidelines will allow you to meet your obligations and still leave you money for investments, charitable giving, vacations, and other expenses.

Debt Guideline #1: Your Total Debt Payment

Your total debt payments, including your mortgage payment, should not exceed 30 percent of your take-home pay.

Debt Guideline #2: Buying Your Home

One of the biggest mistakes you can make is buying a home that is too expensive. Typically, mortgage bankers will allow your mortgage payments to equal approximately 35 percent of your take-home pay. This is considered the maximum amount banks can safely lend without eventually having to foreclose on the home. However, spending 35 percent of your take-home pay on mortgage payments will strain your budget and not leave enough free cash flow to easily meet other living expenses.

Your total house payment, including taxes and insurance, should not exceed 25 percent of your take-home pay. The ideal home mortgage payment falls somewhere between 15 percent and 25 percent of take-home pay.

If you have a high degree of job security and you expect your income to steadily go up, you can use the 25 percent figure. However, 20 percent is the ideal maximum for most people. At 20 percent, you'll have money left over to meet other lifestyle expenses as well as savings and investment needs.

Use 15 percent if you are more conservative and cautious or are uncertain about your job security.

DEBT GUIDELINE #3: BUYING AUTOMOBILES

You'll probably spend more money buying cars than on any other consumer purchase, including homes, over your lifetime. You should strive to avoid a lifetime of auto loans.

Do not finance automobiles for more than 24 months. Let the payments you can afford over 24 months determine how much you can afford to spend on a car.

At the end of that 24 months, continue to make your car payments—to yourself, into an investment account. Continue to make payments to yourself while you drive your current car. When you have accumulated enough money to pay cash for your next car, then buy another car. By continuing this process throughout your life, you will eliminate car payments and the interest expense associated with them.

DEBT GUIDELINE #4: INSTALLMENT DEBT FOR CONSUMER PURCHASES

Purchases bought on installment payments include furniture, appliances, and home repairs such as a new roof or furnace.

For surprises such as a furnace gone bad, you should have an emergency fund. For all other consumer purchases you should save until you have enough money to pay cash. When these two solutions are not practical, use the following guideline for borrowing.

Installment debt payments should not exceed 12–24 months. Smaller purchases, such as a washer/dryer, should be paid off within 12 months. Larger items, such as a new furnace or roof, may take 24 months.

DEBT GUIDELINE #5: CREDIT CARDS

You've read about credit cards in Lesson 4, and hopefully understand their drawbacks and how difficult it is to pay off credit card debt. When you write a check for a purchase, you deduct the expenditure from your balance. The result is that you always know exactly where you stand. This accounting does not take place when you use your credit card.

You cannot afford to pay 18–21 percent interest on any amount of money. Therefore, you must pay off your credit charges at the end of each month. As you learned in Lesson 4, the best way to avoid credit card problems is to enter your credit card charges directly into your checkbook register and subtract the balance just as you would a check. Think of your credit cards as part of your overall checkbook system.

SUMMARY GUIDELINES FOR USING DEBT

To achieve financial independence, you must take control of your debt by staying within these guidelines:

- Home mortgage payments should not exceed 25 percent of your take-home pay.

- Other debt payments should not exceed 15 percent of your take-home pay.

- Your total combined debt payments (mortgage and consumer loans) should not exceed 30 percent of your take-home pay. For example, if your mortgage payment equals 20 percent of your take-home pay, you must limit other debt to 10 percent so that total debt payments do not exceed 30 percent of your take-home pay.

In this lesson, you learned the true cost of borrowing and what guidelines to use when you must borrow. In the next lesson, you learn a step-by-step system that will enable you to "explode" your way out of debt.

EXPLODE YOUR WAY OUT OF DEBT

In this lesson, you learn a fast way to get out of debt using the Debt Pyramid Reduction Strategy.

UNDERSTANDING THE DEBT PYRAMID

If you have debt problems, you'll probably find that you have "stacked up" your various kinds of loans, from mortgages to credit cards. The result resembles a pyramid:

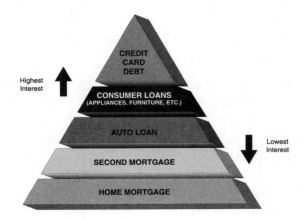

Highest Interest

Lowest Interest

CREDIT CARD DEBT

CONSUMER LOANS
(APPLIANCES, FURNITURE, ETC.)

AUTO LOAN

SECOND MORTGAGE

HOME MORTGAGE

SIX STEPS TO BECOMING DEBT-FREE: THE DEBT PYRAMID REDUCTION STRATEGY

You must commit yourself to the task of becoming debt-free. You must develop a focused plan, get organized, and prioritize if you are to be successful. By following the six-step Debt Pyramid Reduction Strategy that's explained in the following sections, you move methodically and swiftly toward becoming debt-free without sabotaging your lifestyle.

STEP 1: STOP BORROWING

The first step to getting out of debt is to make a commitment to not create any *new* debt. You must immediately stop making any purchases on credit and buy everything with cash. This will require careful budgeting (see Lesson 3).

STEP 2: PRIORITIZE YOUR DEBTS

This step serves to prioritize your debts so that you can easily identify which are the most expensive. The following table shows the Individual Debt Information Report. Use one form for each debt you have.

Organize your Individual Debt Information Reports in order of highest interest rate to lowest interest rate. In the PRIORITY CODE section, number your debts: #1 represents the debt you owe with the highest interest rate, #2 is the debt with the next highest interest rate, and so on. At this point, you should decide if you want to accelerate the payoff of your home mortgage. You may want to be debt-free with the exception of your house payments.

INDIVIDUAL DEBT INFORMATION REPORT (Use One Page for Each Debt)

PRIORITY CODE_____

Account_____

Account Number_____

Current Balance $_____

Interest Rate   _____%

Current Month	Minimum Payment +	Additional Payment =	Total Payment	Balance or # Payments Remaining
_____	$_____	$_____	$_____	$_____
_____	$_____	$_____	$_____	$_____
_____	$_____	$_____	$_____	$_____
_____	$_____	$_____	$_____	$_____
_____	$_____	$_____	$_____	$_____
_____	$_____	$_____	$_____	$_____
_____	$_____	$_____	$_____	$_____
_____	$_____	$_____	$_____	$_____
_____	$_____	$_____	$_____	$_____
_____	$_____	$_____	$_____	$_____
_____	$_____	$_____	$_____	$_____
_____	$_____	$_____	$_____	$_____
_____	$_____	$_____	$_____	$_____

STEP 3: ORGANIZE

Complete the following Debt Summary Worksheet. This process organizes your individual debt summaries from Step 2 so that these debts are listed from the highest interest rate to the lowest interest rate.

DEBT SUMMARY WORKSHEET

PRIORITY CODE	ACCOUNT NAME	INTEREST RATE	CURRENT BALANCE	MINIMUM PAYMENT
1	_____	_____	_____	_____
2	_____	_____	_____	_____
3	_____	_____	_____	_____
4	_____	_____	_____	_____
5	_____	_____	_____	_____
6	_____	_____	_____	_____
7	_____	_____	_____	_____
8	_____	_____	_____	_____
9	_____	_____	_____	_____
10	_____	_____	_____	_____
11	_____	_____	_____	_____
12	_____	_____	_____	_____
13	_____	_____	_____	_____
14	_____	_____	_____	_____
15	_____	_____	_____	_____
Totals			_____	_____

Amount available for extra monthly payments (for example, $100.00/mo.) =_____

Total amount allocated to debt reduction each month = $_____*

This is the amount you will apply toward all your debt until you are completely debt-free.

Add up your minimum payments. Determine whether your budget will allow you to pay any amount each month above the minimum monthly payments (say, $100 a month). This additional amount, plus the total amount of your minimum monthly payments, becomes your total debt reduction payment. **This payment amount will not change until you are completely out of debt!**

STEP 4: RAISE CASH BY DOING AN ASSET REVIEW

You may have assets that can be sold to raise cash. Items that you don't want or need may be of value to someone else. You can often earn several hundred dollars or more by cleaning out your home and having a garage sale. Not only do you benefit from the cash, but you also feel good about cleaning out your closets and garage. Do you have boats, bikes, or motorcycles you can sell? Do you have an extra car, or do you really need two cars? You might even consider buying a less expensive home.

Raise all the cash you can from these sources. The cash raised should be paid on your #1 priority debt.

STEP 5: LOWER THE INTEREST RATE ON YOUR DEBTS BY CONSOLIDATING YOUR LOANS

If possible, consolidate your debts into lower interest rate loans. This is not a typical consolidation loan. You only want to consolidate if you can get a lower interest rate. Remember, you are not to increase the amount of money you are borrowing (Step 1), but rather, you're consolidating loans you already have into a lower interest rate.

Consolidation Loan   Many loan companies offer debt consolidation loans, meaning they will consolidate many or all of your debts into one loan, with a payment that's less than what you are currently paying. The problem with the typical consolidation loan is that you're charged a very high rate of interest. The reason your payment is lower is because the loan company extends the term over which your payments are made. You should avoid these types of high interest rate loans if possible.

tip   Before you attempt to consolidate your loans, check your credit history by contacting your local credit bureau. There will be a small charge of $10–$20. Any potential lender will review your credit history before making you a loan, so you want to know in advance the information they will see. If your credit history is bad, you'll want to discuss it with potential lenders before they find out on their own. Also, it's not unusual to find a mistake in your credit history file. If you do find a mistake, correct it before you apply for your loan.

Check out the following loan sources:

- *Cash Value Life Insurance.* You may have a life insurance policy that has built up cash values. Normally, you can borrow these funds at very low interest rates of from 5 to 8 percent. If you have such a policy, contact your agent to get the details on how much you can borrow and the interest rates.

- *Home Equity.* If you own your home, you may be eligible for a home equity loan. Interest rates on these loans are usually very favorable, and the interest is tax deductible. However, there's a significant risk to taking out a home equity loan. If you can't make your payments, you could lose your home to foreclosure. Also, closing expenses—such as appraisals, title insurance, and surveys—can be as high as several hundred dollars.

tip

Shop around. Since many banks offer home equity loans, you should look for one with the most advantageous features—a low interest rate and the fewest fees.

- *Retirement Account.* Many company retirement plans have loan provisions that enable you to borrow against your holdings. The amount you can borrow is always a percentage of your account balance, such as 50 percent. Generally, you'll pay a relatively low interest rate. Also, the payback schedule is often lenient, sometimes as long as 60 months.

- *Loans from Family Members.* Family members with idle cash that isn't earning much interest may be willing to loan you money. There are laws governing loans between family members, so be sure to talk with your accountant or a financial planner before taking a loan from someone in your family.

- *Low Interest Rate Credit Cards.* Many credit cards feature hefty 18–21 percent interest charges. But today's competitive credit card market has led to lower interest rates on many cards. For a list of competitive credit card issuers, contact CardTrak at Box 1700, Frederick, Maryland 21702, by phone at 800-344-7714, or on the Internet at http://www.ramresearch.com. A survey listing hundreds of banks is updated monthly. It costs $5, payable by check or credit card.

 Most credit card companies allow you to transfer your account balance from your old card to your new card.

STEP 6: IMPLEMENT YOUR STRATEGIES

Pull out your Debt Summary Worksheet (Step 3). Pay the maximum that you can pay on your #1 priority debt while paying the minimum on all other debts. When your #1 debt is paid off, take the amount you were paying on #1 and add it to the minimum payment on #2 on your Debt Summary Worksheet. Continue this strategy until all your debts are paid off.

 The total amount you pay each month will not change, even though your minimum payments may be going down and individual debts are being paid off. This is *the key* to the Debt Pyramid Reduction Strategy.

Getting out of debt is a worthy goal. By applying discipline and implementing the Debt Pyramid Reduction Strategy, you can put yourself on the fast track to becoming debt-free.

In this lesson, you learned about the Debt Pyramid Reduction Strategy, an organized, methodical system to get you out of debt fast. In the next lesson, you learn whether you need life insurance and how to select from the various types of life insurance policies.

7

UNDERSTANDING LIFE INSURANCE

In this lesson, you learn whether you need life insurance, and what the differences are between the various types of life insurance.

THE PURPOSE OF LIFE INSURANCE

Buying life insurance can be very confusing, but you can demystify the process by first understanding what the purpose of life insurance is. It is simply to replace income for your dependents.

If your salary is necessary to support your spouse or children, when you die, your life insurance would be used as a source of funds to continue providing income for your dependents.

While this may be a simple concept, life insurance has become one of the most complicated financial products sold today. And life insurance salespeople are among the most persuasive sales-people around.

As a result, it's easy to end up over-insured, under-insured, or with the wrong type of insurance. To avoid getting the wrong amount or type of life insurance, you must first understand the basic types of life insurance.

TYPES OF LIFE INSURANCE

Although life insurance policies come in many shapes and sizes, all life insurance falls into one of two categories: term insurance or cash value insurance.

Term insurance is "pure" insurance. You pay a premium, which covers you for a certain period of time. If you die during that period of time, your beneficiary collects the face amount of the policy. If you don't die, you don't get any money back and you must "renew" the insurance by paying an additional premium if you want the coverage to continue.

Premium   A premium is insurance jargon for what you pay the insurer so you will be covered under its policy for a certain period of time.

Cash value insurance is term insurance with a savings feature. In addition to the term premium, called *mortality reserves*, you give the insurance company extra money, which it invests for you. Later, you can use some of this extra money by taking out a loan, or in some cases, a withdrawal. At the time of your death, your beneficiary receives the term insurance plus the savings account.

For a more complete look at your life insurance options, you should review the various term insurance and cash value insurance policies.

TERM INSURANCE

Term insurance plans are typically sold as either annual renewable term insurance or level term insurance.

With annual renewable term insurance, each year your insurance company sends you a bill that is higher than the prior year's bill. This is because as you get older, you are statistically more likely to die.

With level term insurance, your premium stays the same for a stated period of time, typically 5, 10, 15, or 20 years. The longer the period of time, the higher your premiums. At the end of the stated period, you have a guaranteed right to renew the policy regardless of your health condition, but for a significantly higher premium. Many companies offer a lower renewal rate if you are willing to provide proof that you are still in good health by taking a physical exam. See the following table for comparable premiums during the first 5 years.

YEAR	ANNUAL RENEWABLE TERM	10-YEAR LEVEL TERM	15-YEAR LEVEL TERM	20-YEAR LEVEL TERM
1	$182	$202	$222	$264
2	$214	$202	$222	$264
3	$226	$202	$222	$264
4	$240	$202	$222	$264
5	$264	$202	$222	$264

Source: 1st Colonial Life. These term rates are for a male, age 30, in excellent health.

CASH VALUE INSURANCE

As with term insurance, there are also various types of cash value insurance. Three of the most popular types are:

- *Whole Life.* Whole Life insurance has been around for a long time. With whole life insurance, you commit to a fixed premium, which includes the term insurance charge plus the savings feature. The insurance company takes the savings portion of your premium and invests it for you in the general assets of the insurance company, which includes real estate, commercial mortgages, bonds, and, to a limited extent, stocks. You receive a guaranteed rate of return, usually ranging from 4 to 4 1/2 percent, and in many cases, dividends, which are declared by the Board of Directors.

- *Universal Life.* Universal Life insurance became popular in the 1980s, when interest rates were very high. With this type of policy, your savings are invested in interest-sensitive investments such as certificates of deposit, commercial paper, and bonds. You are notified periodically of the interest earned on your savings. Also, unlike whole life policies, you pay flexible rather than fixed premiums. You must pay an amount that covers the term insurance premiums, but the insurance company allows you to vary the amount you contribute toward the savings program.

- *Variable Life.* Variable Life insurance is the newest type of life insurance. As mutual funds became increasingly popular, insurance companies developed a life insurance product that uses mutual funds. You must pay your term insurance charge, but you can then direct your savings into various mutual funds offered by the insurance company. The company typically offers a variety of choices, such as stock funds, bond funds, money market funds, and guaranteed interest rate contracts, which are similar to certificates of deposit. You make the decision about which funds to invest in, and you are allowed to make changes from time to time.

WHO NEEDS LIFE INSURANCE?

Before choosing a particular type of life insurance, you should ask whether you need life insurance at all. Remember, the purpose of life insurance is to provide income for dependents. If you don't have someone dependent on you for his or her financial support, you don't need life insurance.

Here are some specific situations:

- *You are single without children.* Most single people have no dependents and therefore have no need for life insurance.

- *You are married without children.* If both you and your spouse work, in all likelihood neither of you is financially dependent on the other. Again, no life insurance is necessary. If one spouse is unemployed, you may need some life insurance to provide a bridge of income until the other person can acquire the training or education necessary to get a good job. You may also need life insurance to cover a portion of joint debts, such as a mortgage, that are being paid from both incomes.

- *You are married with children.* If you have dependents, consider your life insurance needs carefully. You will need to buy enough insurance to maintain a similar lifestyle for your surviving family (see Lesson 8, "How Much Life Insurance Is Enough?").

 Insurance on children   Unless your child is a movie star, it's unlikely that you or anyone else is dependent on them for financial support. It's therefore not necessary to buy life insurance for your children.

WHICH KIND OF INSURANCE SHOULD YOU BUY?

Most newlyweds should buy term insurance rather than cash value insurance. Here are two reasons why:

- *Premiums.* Cash value insurance premiums are four to ten times more costly than term premiums. For example, a $250,000 whole life insurance policy on a man, age 30, costs $2,105 per year with one company. The same amount of 10-year, level term insurance costs $268 per year with that same company.

- *Penalties for quitting.* Most cash value policies have significant penalties if you quit within the first 10–20 years. These penalties can be as much as 100 percent of the premiums that you have already paid. Not only would you lose your term insurance premium contributions, but you also would lose your savings! Why? Because most of your money went to pay high commissions to the salesperson, as well as to cover company expenses.

Again, if you do need life insurance, you should probably purchase term insurance in an adequate amount to protect your dependents.

In this lesson, you learned that you should buy life insurance only if you have dependents who would suffer financially in the event of your death. You also learned why term insurance is probably the best choice for you. In the next lesson, you learn how to determine the right amount of life insurance you should buy.

How Much Life Insurance Is Enough?

Determining how much life insurance you should own need not be a daunting task. In this lesson, you learn how to determine how much life insurance you need to buy and also how to find the best deals from the more than 2,000 insurance companies.

How Much Life Insurance Do You Need?

If you asked ten people how much coverage you need, you'd probably get ten different answers. However, there's an easy three-step process that provides a simple yet logical approach to answering this important question.

If you are married and have no children, you need only enough life insurance to pay off any joint debts. However, if you have children, your need for life insurance increases substantially. Use the following three-step process to determine your life insurance needs (use Table 8.1 for your worksheet):

1. If you are the sole income provider, multiply your total annual income by .80. (If both you and your spouse work, combine both incomes and multiply by .80.) This results in reducing your income by 20 percent. The reason you do this is because there is one less spender in the household (you!).

2. Divide your answer in Step 1 by the rate of return you would reasonably expect to earn on the life insurance proceeds once they are invested. Your answer here indicates how much money you will need in order to continue providing the necessary income to your surviving family.

3. Subtract any savings or investments you already have from your answer in Step 2. This is the amount of life insurance you should own.

Consider these two examples:

John and Mary Smith have two children. John earns $50,000 a year and Mary stays home to raise the children. The couple have $25,000 in personal investments; they assume that they could earn 7.5 percent on investments.

1. Multiply John's income by .80 ($50,000 × .80 = $40,000).

2. Divide $40,000 by their expected rate of return 7.5 percent on invested money ($40,000 ÷ .075 = $533,333). This amount of money invested at 7.5 percent will provide the needed $40,000 per year for Mary and the children.

3. Subtract their current savings and investments ($25,000) from $533,333 ($533,333 - $25,000 = $508,333). This is the amount of life insurance John needs to buy.

If both John and Mary work, the example changes. Their total income is $65,000, but John's earnings are $30,000 and Mary's earnings are $35,000. To see how much life insurance John needs, perform the following calculations:

1. Multiply the family's income of $65,000 by .80 ($65,000 × .80 = $52,000). Again, the survivors' income need is reduced because John is no longer a spender. Since Mary plans to continue working, subtract her income also ($52,000 - $35,000 = $17,000). This $17,000 represents the income that needs to be replaced upon John's death.

2. Divide $17,000 by the couple's expected rate of return (7.5 percent) ($17,000 ÷ .075 = $226,667).

3. Subtract their current investments ($25,000) from $226,667 ($226,667 - $25,000 = $201,667). This is the amount of life insurance needed on John.

Because the family also depends on Mary's income, you would now need to complete this exercise for her.

Table 8.1

Life Insurance Needs Worksheet

Step 1.	Your family income (annually)	$
	Discount factor	x ___.80
	Total income needed by surviving family =	$
Step 1b.	Subtract surviving spouse's annual income	−
	Surviving family income need from outside sources =	$ ___
Step 2.	Divide your estimated rate of return on invested assets into answer in Step 1b	÷ ___
	Equals the total amount of money needed to provide for your survivors =	$
Step 3.	Subtract your current savings and investments	− ___
	Equals total life insurance needed =	$

Use the preceding table to calculate your own life insurance needs. You should use your answer from Table 8.1 as a rule of thumb and then personalize the amount of life insurance you need, according to your particular situation. For example, you may want to increase the amount of insurance to help cover the costs of college expenses for your children. Or, you may want additional insurance to pay off some of your debts. If your goal is to provide a lifetime income for your dependents, additional insurance will be needed to offset the ravages of inflation.

tip   The federal government provides a Social Security Survivors Benefit to help surviving spouses with small children. To determine the level of income for which you are eligible, call the Social Security Administration (800-772-1213) and request the form "Record of Earnings and Estimate of Benefits Statement." After you complete this form and return it to the Social Security Administration, you will get a summary of your benefits. Think of these benefits as extra money; don't use them as part of your calculation to determine your life insurance needs. Remember, these benefits end when your youngest child reaches age 18.

INSURANCE ON A HOMEMAKER

If you have young children, replacing the services of a homemaker can be quite expensive. Ask yourself whether you can afford to pay someone to perform these services if your homemaker spouse were to die. If you're fortunate enough to have a family member who could step in and help, you wouldn't need insurance. On the other hand, if you believe you should get life insurance to cover these services, a $100,000 to $200,000 term policy should provide adequate coverage. By buying a 10- to 15-year level term insurance policy, you will provide coverage until the children are old enough to assist with their own care.

GETTING THE BEST LIFE INSURANCE DEAL

For most newlyweds, term insurance is a smarter choice than cash value insurance. Fortunately for the consumer, term insurance is also a very competitive product. In terms of planning and budgeting, 10-, 15-, or 20-year level term is advised. That way you have a predictable premium for a fixed period of time.

There are a few companies that specialize in helping consumers shop for the best rates, such as the following:

Wholesale Insurance Network (800) 808-5810

Insurance Clearinghouse (800) 522-2827

Insurance Information Inc. (800) 472-5800

To get the best deal, first decide how much life insurance you need and what kind of term insurance best fits your circumstances. For example, if you decide that you need $300,000 of 10-year level term life insurance, call one or two of the companies listed above. If you have a local agent, ask him or her for a quote. A simple comparison will ensure that you get the best deal.

In this lesson, you learned a logical way to figure out how much insurance you need to have and how to get the best deal. In the next lesson, you learn what you can do to reduce your car insurance premium by as much as 50 percent.

9

Automobile Insurance: Slash Your Costs by 20–50 Percent

In this lesson, you learn what coverage is necessary for your automobile and how you can reduce your car insurance costs by 20–50 percent.

Cutting Your Automobile Insurance Costs

Your automobile insurance premiums are determined by four main factors:

- The type of car you own
- Your driving record
- Your policy limits and coverage
- The deductible you choose

If you want to control your expenses in this area, pay attention to all four factors.

THE TYPE OF CAR YOU OWN

Expensive cars cost more to insure than inexpensive cars because repair costs are generally higher. Also, smaller cars carry higher premiums than larger cars because smaller cars typically sustain more damage in an accident. Sports cars cost more to insure than sedans because sports cars are costlier to repair. Foreign or unusual cars cost more as there are fewer mechanics who can repair these cars.

As a car gets older, its premiums go down because there is less value to insure. Also, certain car models that are "theft targets" carry higher premiums.

Before you buy your next car, discuss the insurance costs with your insurance agent. Insurance costs of different models will vary widely. If you currently own a model with unusually high premiums, it may be worthwhile to change the car you drive. Since insurance costs less on older models, you should consider a used car.

YOUR DRIVING RECORD

More than anything else, a poor driving record will dramatically affect your premiums as well as your ability to get insurance at all. If you have a bad driving record, there is not much you can do but slow down and wait. After about five years, your record will be erased. You should also try shopping around. Some insurance companies are more tolerant of drivers with bad records than other companies.

tip   The more of your business a company has, the more lenient the insurer is likely to be if you have an accident or moving violation. Consider carrying your homeowners and auto insurance with the same company.

Your Policy Limits and Coverage

All automobile policies contain six types of coverage: Collision, Comprehensive, Bodily Injury Liability, Property Damage Liability, Medical Payments, and Uninsured and Underinsured Motorist.

- *Collision Coverage.* This coverage pays to repair your car if you have an accident. It will also pay to repair your car if it is damaged by someone who doesn't have adequate insurance. Collision coverage represents a major component of your automobile insurance premium.

  You can reduce costs by carefully selecting the type of car you buy. Check with your agent for car types with low collision premiums. An example is cars with anti-lock brakes. The anti-lock braking system is far superior to traditional braking systems. Cars with anti-lock brakes are involved in fewer accidents.

- *Comprehensive Coverage (also known as "Other than Collision Coverage").* This covers everything other than collision damage such as vandalism, theft, glass breakage, fire, flood, and hitting an animal.

 Many policies will pay 100 percent of the cost to repair windshield "dings." If your windshield becomes damaged, have it repaired before it becomes a crack and must be replaced. If the windshield has to be replaced, your deductible will apply. Call your agent for details.

- *Bodily Injury Liability Coverage.* This is important coverage that pays if you have injured or killed someone in an accident. You shouldn't try to cut corners on this coverage. This coverage needs to be high enough so that the victim, or his or her dependents, doesn't go after your personal assets after collecting the insurance money. Even if you have few or no assets, don't assume you are "judgment-proof." There have been cases where the courts have awarded victims a "garnishment" of wages. Consider a minimum of $50,000 to $100,000 of coverage.

Garnishment   Garnishment is when a court of law requires someone's employer to withhold a portion of his salary in order to make payments to a victim.

- *Property Damage Liability Coverage.* This coverage pays for damage your car causes to another person's car or property. Your coverage here should be at least $50,000.

- *Medical Payments Coverage.* This covers you and your passengers for doctor and hospital-related bills that are the result of an accident that is your fault.

  Your health insurance must be used first before your automobile medical payments coverage can be used. This is what is known as "double coverage." If you have existing medical coverage, you may want to reduce medical payment coverage to a minimum level ($500–$1,000) or drop it altogether.

- *Uninsured and Underinsured Motorist Coverage.* Some people drive with little or no automobile insurance coverage. If you are hit by one of these people, your uninsured motorist coverage pays all items that you would have been able to collect from the negligent party. This includes medical expenses, lost wages, and possibly "pain and suffering." If you have medical and disability income insurance, you must use it first before you can

collect under your uninsured motorist coverage. You
cannot collect twice. If you do have good medical, life,
and disability income insurance, you may want to reduce or eliminate your uninsured motorist coverage.

tip   If you drop uninsured or underinsured motorist
coverage, you give up the ability to collect for pain
and suffering from your insurance company.

THE DEDUCTIBLE YOU CHOOSE

The best way to reduce your insurance premium is to select
the right deductible. Remember, your goal is to insure only
catastrophic losses. By increasing your deductible from $100
to $500, you may cut premiums by as much as 30 percent.
Generally, the best deductible for most people is $500. But
consider $1,000 if you can afford that much out-of-pocket
expense. Going from $500 to $1,000 should save you another
5–10 percent. The deductible applies to both collision and
comprehensive coverage. Normally, the savings will be more
dramatic for the collision portion of your coverage.

tip   Avoid small claims. Some automobile insurance
companies will raise your rates after just one claim.
Your best solution is to self-insure the small claims
by raising your deductible to $500 or $1,000.

COVERAGE YOU CAN DO WITHOUT

In addition to the basic coverage that you need, insurance companies add a list of extra coverage that you can buy but don't

need. Car rental, stolen radio, accidental death, weekly disability, and towing coverage don't cost much, but aren't necessary. These items should be well within your ability to self-insure.

 If you are totally reliant on your car, the car rental coverage may be appropriate.

AUTOMOBILE INSURANCE DISCOUNTS

Insurance companies often offer discounts on your premiums. Contact your agent or company to determine what discounts they offer and if you are eligible.

GETTING THE BEST DEAL ON AUTOMOBILE INSURANCE

Automobile insurance is a competitive business. You can save money by doing your homework. First, you should decide what coverage is appropriate for you. Then, you should shop around for the best deal.

Premiums can vary widely from company to company, so you should get quotes from at least three companies. Good sources are State Farm, Geico, Allstate, or any independent agent.

 If you were an officer in the military, contact USAA at (800) 531-8080. This company has some of the best automobile insurance rates in the country for veterans.

Be sure to compare identical coverage from each insurer. Before you choose the lowest premium, you should also find out how a company treats a single accident or ticket. Some companies will raise your premiums significantly for one accident or ticket. Others may drop you after a small number of claims. Being "branded" a bad risk will make it harder to get competitive insurance in the future.

Remember, you want to self-insure as much as you can. Use insurance to cover large losses only. By implementing all of these strategies, you should be able to cut your premiums 20–50 percent while maintaining adequate coverage.

PERSONAL LIABILITY UMBRELLA COVERAGE

If you're concerned about your potential liability, you should consider buying a Personal Liability Umbrella policy. This policy covers you for liability over and above your automobile and homeowners liability. It also includes additional coverage for slander. While this policy is inexpensive—less than $300 per year for $1,000,000 of coverage—it requires that you raise your automobile liability coverage to $300,000 or $500,000. You must also raise your homeowners liability coverage to $300,000. If your assets exceed $100,000, you should definitely consider adding an umbrella policy.

tip   When buying a personal liability umbrella policy, be sure to talk to your automobile and homeowners agent(s). The requirements for underlying limits vary from company to company.

In this lesson, you learned how to evaluate your automobile insurance coverage and make the changes necessary to minimize your premiums while getting adequate coverage. In the next lesson, you learn how to choose the right homeowners or renters insurance.

Personal Property and Homeowners Insurance: How to Save 10–20 Percent

In this lesson, you learn how to find the best property and homeowners coverage, and how to cut your insurance premiums by as much as 20 percent.

What Is Homeowners Coverage?

Homeowners insurance covers theft, vandalism, liability (if someone is injured while on your property), fire, and so forth. Your home is your single biggest asset, and you must insure it. However, by carefully evaluating the coverage you need, you can save significantly on your premium cost.

When you evaluate homeowners insurance, you should focus on three main types of coverage:

- Dwelling coverage
- Personal property coverage
- Liability coverage

To save money, you should pay only for coverage you need and eliminate the extras.

DWELLING COVERAGE

Dwelling coverage includes damage to your home or other structures on your property, such as a toolshed or garage. You need enough insurance to cover the replacement value of the house itself.

 Replacement Value Replacement value refers to the construction cost to rebuild your home. Don't confuse this with the market value of your home, which includes land, driveways, landscaping, location, and so forth.

KEEPING YOUR DWELLING COVERAGE CURRENT

It is your responsibility to make certain you maintain adequate coverage. Since construction prices constantly rise, the replacement cost of your home will also increase. Contact your company or agent every two or three years to determine if you need to raise your coverage amount. To help address this problem, some companies now offer an "inflation guard" provision that automatically increases your coverage each year, based on an inflation index.

 If you remodel or add on to your home, you must contact your company or agent and have your coverage limits raised to cover the increase in replacement costs.

PERSONAL PROPERTY COVERAGE

This covers damage to, or loss of, your personal property anywhere in the world, with some exclusions (such as your car). *Personal property* includes any items you own, such as cameras, clothes, appliances, televisions, jewelry, and furniture.

The amount of Personal Property coverage you have is determined as a percentage of your Dwelling Coverage, typically 50–70 percent. In most cases, this is more than adequate.

tip   Make certain you have "Replacement Value" coverage versus "Cash Value" coverage. Suppose someone steals your 10-year old 21-inch color television. If you have Replacement Value coverage, the insurance adjuster will pay you based on what it costs to buy a new 21-inch color television. Under Cash Value coverage, you would be paid based on the estimated value of your 10-year old television—less than $50. Replacement Value is worth the additional cost.

LIABILITY COVERAGE

This coverage is designed to pay if you are found liable in a situation in which property damage or personal injury to others occurs. Due to the frequency of lawsuits and the size of judgments being awarded, you should consider carrying liability limits of at least $100,000 to $300,000.

Liability coverage is normally restricted to claims inside the United States and Canada. Also, it does not cover every incidence of liability. Discuss this coverage with your agent.

If you have a swimming pool, consider raising your liability insurance to $500,000 or more. You may even want to add an umbrella policy (discussed in lesson 9).

CHOOSING THE BEST POLICY

For homeowners and property coverage, consider these policies:

- HO-3, also known as a Special Form policy, covers "all risks" on your home, and "broad form" on your personal property. *All risks* is insurance jargon meaning everything is covered unless it is specifically excluded. *Broad form* means all items and perils that are covered are specifically listed in the policy.

  The difference between all risks and broad form is that under all risks the burden of proof is on the insurance company. The insurer must prove that your claim is specifically excluded in the policy. Under broad form, the burden of proof is on you; you must prove your claim is specifically included in the policy. Obviously, all risks favors the consumer.

  HO-3 is the most popular form of homeowners coverage and is the best value for most people.

- HO-5, also known as a Comprehensive Form or an All Risks policy, insures all risks to your home and personal property unless it is specifically excluded. This is the most comprehensive and expensive coverage, but should be considered by those people who have substantial personal property assets. Have your agent compare the features and costs of the HO-3 and the HO-5 policies.

For Renters

Renters insurance is generally inexpensive, yet many renters do not have coverage. The fact that you don't own the building you live in does not mean that you don't need insurance. An HO-4 policy covers tenants' contents and liability. Be sure contents are covered at replacement value rather than cash value. You also want Additional Living Expenses coverage, if available. It pays the expenses of living somewhere else if your apartment becomes uninhabitable.

For Condominium Owners

HO-6 for condominium owners is similar to HO-4 for renters. As a condominium owner, you are responsible for your personal property and may be liable if someone is injured while he or she is in your condo. You will need insurance to protect yourself and your property.

Getting Discounts

As with automobile insurance, a range of discounts are available on your homeowners insurance. Contact your agent or insurance company to see what discounts you can qualify for. Often, something as simple as adding smoke detectors will reduce your premiums.

Getting the Best Deal

There are four keys to getting the best deal on your homeowners insurance:

- *Select your deductible.* The deductible is the amount you pay before the insurance company pays. It can be as little as $50 or as much as $1,000. One of the best ways to reduce your premiums is to raise your deductible. Generally, a $500 deductible is the best value. But if you can afford a deductible of $1,000, you should do so.

 Avoid small claims. Insurance companies don't like to handle small claims and will cancel your insurance if you turn in too many small claims. Self-insure the small things by raising your deductible to $500 or $1,000.

- *Choose the right coverage.* Decide what coverage best suits your needs. For most people, an HO-3 policy is appropriate.

- *Decline optional types of coverage.* All companies offer optional types of coverage for increased premiums. Options include coverage for stolen credit cards; temporary repairs to prevent further damage; fire department surcharges; damaged property removal; and damage to scrubs, trees, and plants. You can do without most of these optional types of coverage. While the added premiums are not large, you will be paying for them for a lifetime. Remember, the insurance company makes money on all of these optional types of coverage.

- *Shop around for the best prices.* As you may have guessed, homeowners premiums can vary widely. After you decide on the type of policy, deductible, and riders you want, you are ready to begin shopping.

Contact an independent agent in your community. They represent several companies and are paid by commissions.

You also want to get a quote from at least one direct writer. A *direct writer* is someone who represents only one company and is paid by commissions. Good choices are State Farm and Allstate.

Finally, get a quote from a captive carrier. A *captive carrier* is a company without field agents. You deal directly with the company through a toll-free telephone number. Their representatives are paid salaries instead of commissions. A good choice is Geico (800-841-3000). For military officers and their family members, contact USAA at (800-531-8080).

To locate insurance companies or agents in your area, check your yellow pages under Insurance or ask for recommendations from friends, neighbors, and co-workers.

IF YOU HAVE TO FILE A CLAIM

You want to reap full benefits if you have a claim. Consider the worst-case scenario: Your home and everything in it is completely destroyed by fire. This situation creates several common problems that can be solved with a little bit of pre-planning.

Problem #1: When you file your claim, your first problem is remembering all the items of personal property. The insurance company will only pay you for what you can list. Can you remember, for example, all the books on your bookshelf or all your knickknacks?

Solution: The solution is to videotape all of your personal possessions. Go from room to room and don't forget to record what is in drawers, closets, and storage rooms. Make comments as you go; include descriptions, purchase prices, and values, if you know them. The key is to include every item, whether large or small in value. The little things can add up to thousands of dollars. Be sure to update your videotape periodically as you make new purchases.

Problem #2: The next problem you face is proving the value of the destroyed items to the insurance company. For example, the prices of dining room furniture vary widely. A videotape alone may not tell the whole story.

Solution: Keep a file of the receipts for all major items you purchase. Be sure to identify what each receipt is for ("This receipt is for the living room rocking chair.").

 tip   Store the videotape and inventory file folder away from home. A good place is at work or at the home of a relative. Be sure someone outside your immediate family knows where these items are kept.

Problem #3: Most policies apply special limits to certain types of property. These include such things as jewelry, silverware, cash, coin collections, fine art, and so forth. For example, jewelry claims may be limited to $1,000. If you have jewelry worth $3,000, and it is stolen, you will only be reimbursed $1,000.

Solution: Purchase a special "articles floater" rider to insure important items that you would want to replace if lost or stolen. You usually will have to get an appraisal of value for the insurance company. Also, no deductible applies to claims on these riders.

tip   You can't afford to insure everything. Insure only those expensive items that you feel you would have to replace if lost or stolen.

Problem #4: Most policies provide little or no coverage for business equipment, computers, or liability associated with an office at home.

Solution: Contact your agent regarding an Incidental Business rider to cover these items.

In this lesson, you learned how to choose the best homeowners insurance, and how to reduce your premiums by 10–20 percent. You also learned how to maximize your reimbursement if you have a claim. In the next lesson, you learn about two other types of insurance: health and disability income.

HEALTH AND DISABILITY INCOME INSURANCE

In this lesson, you learn how to evaluate health and disability income insurance policies.

HEALTH INSURANCE

If your employer provides or makes available group health insurance, consider yourself lucky. This insurance is very expensive and the benefits of a group plan include reduced costs and more extensive coverage than that provided by individual plans.

TYPES OF COVERAGE

Coverage falls into two broad categories: Basic Health and Hospitalization and Major Medical.

- Basic Health and Hospitalization covers the cost of hospital stays, nursing services, operating room expenses, simple surgery, x-rays, and so forth.

- Major Medical covers those costs above Basic Health and Hospitalization for major illnesses or accidents. Usually, these plans have no limits on the number of days you spend in the hospital or total expenses for a covered injury or illness, but they do have a lifetime dollar limit, typically one million dollars. However, some policies are unlimited.

CHOOSING THE BEST POLICY

Many large employers offer several plans to choose from. In evaluating the plans, weigh the trade-off between premiums and coverage. The more extensive and flexible the coverage, the more you have to pay in premiums. For employer-contracted group health insurance, look for the following features:

- Lifetime benefit of one million dollars or more. Considering the current costs of treatment for major illness, you could use up one million dollars in benefits quickly. A policy with unlimited benefits is better if it's available.

- Full coverage for all family members from their date of birth until the time they leave home or reach ages 21 to 23.

- Coverage of all room and board costs in a semi-private room with no daily limit.

- No maximum charge per illness.

- Generous maternity coverage if you plan to have children.

- A $1,000 stop loss limit. Most policies split the costs of medical expenses with you. After your deductible, the insurance company pays 80 percent and you pay 20 percent of the bills. A good stop loss provision will limit your out-of-pocket expenses to $1,000 a year.

Saving Money

If you are healthy, the best thing you can do to save money is choose a high annual deductible. Many plans offer a $500 or even $1,000 deductible. If you rarely visit the doctor, this approach will save you money.

 If you use a high deductible, be sure you establish an emergency fund that will easily cover out-of-pocket expenses.

If you plan to have children in the next few years, you may want to take the policy with the best maternity benefits.

If you and your spouse both have access to coverage through your employers, your decision becomes more complicated. One spouse may be better off joining the other spouse's plan. Or you may be better off maintaining separate coverage. Be sure to read the coverage carefully. Don't overlook the "pre-existing conditions" clause in most policies.

 Pre-Existing Conditions   A pre-existing condition clause means that the insurance company will not cover claims for a certain period of time for medical conditions you had prior to joining the plan. For example, if you are a diabetic, you will not receive payment for treatment for diabetes for a stated period of time, usually six months to three years.

Be sure your policy covers newborns from the day of birth. Otherwise, a child born with a birth defect may not be covered. Find out ahead of time the procedure for notifying your insurer that you have a baby to be added to your policy.

INDIVIDUAL HEALTH INSURANCE

If you don't have access to health insurance through your employer, you have two options. First, you may be able to get insurance through a professional or trade organization. For example, if you are an accountant, your state association may provide access to group insurance. Look into any union, club, or professional associations to see if any of them provide group insurance.

Second, if all else fails, you can buy an individual health policy. In addition to the features discussed earlier in this lesson, you want a policy that is guaranteed renewable. This means that the insurance company must continue to renew the policy each year without requiring you to prove that you are still in good health.

Shop around to find the best policy and rates. Ask friends and co-workers or contact several individual agents who specialize in health insurance. Look under Health Insurance or Insurance in the yellow pages.

If you are willing to self-insure the first $1,000 to $2,500 of expenses, you should contact the Insurance Clearinghouse at (800) 522-2827. This group represents numerous insurance companies and will send you several quotes. If you buy insurance through the Clearinghouse, it receives a commission.

If your funds are limited, spend your available money on Major Medical Insurance. It is broader and covers catastrophic illness.

Avoid hospital indemnity policies. These policies typically pay you $50–$100 for every day that you are in the hospital after you have been there a certain number of days, usually seven. These payments supplement any benefits paid by your health or disability income insurance. Assuming that you have good health insurance and disability income insurance, these policies represent a poor value. They are really a short-term disability income insurance policy.

If you stop working and lose your health insurance, you may find it difficult to find new coverage. Under a federal law, COBRA, you are guaranteed the right to maintain your coverage with your existing carrier for a period of 18 months. However, you must apply for coverage within the first 60 days of termination. The purpose of COBRA is to allow sufficient time for people to find new health insurance without having to be uninsured for any period of time.

tip

If you are denied coverage because of a pre-existing condition, check with your state insurance department to find out whether your state sponsors "pooled" health plans for hard-to-insure people. Your state insurance department's phone number is located in the state government section of your phone book.

DISABILITY INCOME INSURANCE

Disability Income insurance is a contract provided by an insurance company whereby they agree to pay you a certain income for a specified period of time should you become disabled through an accident or illness and be unable to work.

WHO NEEDS DISABILITY INCOME INSURANCE?

As a young couple, one important asset is your ability to earn a living. Most people earn more than one million dollars during their working years. Your odds of becoming disabled are far greater than premature death (see the following table).

THE CHANCES OF BEING DISABLED VS. DYING BEFORE AGE 65

AGE	25	30	35	40	45	50	55
	2.8 to 1	2.7 to 1	2.8 to 1	2.5 to 1	2.4 to 1	2.3 to 1	2.2 to 1

Many people live paycheck to paycheck. If your paycheck stops, where will the money come from to pay your bills for the next six months, one year, or five years? If you don't have an answer, most likely you need disability income insurance.

However, there are two possible instances when you may have little or no need for disability income insurance:

- Your spouse has an income substantial enough to pay the family expenses.

- You have accumulated enough income-producing assets as a couple that disability income insurance is not necessary.

HOW MUCH DISABILITY INCOME INSURANCE DO YOU NEED?

A policy that insures from 60 to 70 percent of your income is sufficient because when you become disabled, many expenses are significantly reduced. For example, income taxes and transportation costs will be less.

Two types of disability coverage may be available to you:

- *Group Coverage.* Many larger employers provide group disability income coverage. However, don't assume your employer's coverage is always adequate. Often, group coverage provides limited benefits for a very limited period of time. Compare your group coverage to the recommendations in the "Policy Features You Do Want" section later in this lesson. Also, many trade and professional associations offer group coverage. If you can find good group coverage, it will be your cheapest route.

 tip   If you are relying on group disability benefits, you may need higher coverage because the benefits are subject to income taxes.

- *Individual Coverage.* If group coverage is not available to you, then you need to buy an individual policy. While the cost of an individual disability income insurance policy is significantly higher than a group policy, it does have some advantages. First, it is portable. If you change jobs, it goes with you. With group insurance, if you terminate or are terminated, you lose your coverage. Second, if you become disabled, the benefits you receive are tax-free. Group benefits are taxable if the premiums are paid by your employer. Finally, individual policies offer optional riders, such as cost-of-living increases for benefits.

After you decide how much insurance you need, you should choose your policy features. Disability policies often have options that you don't need and should not pay for.

POLICY FEATURES YOU DO WANT

When you're buying individual insurance, you can save money by following these guidelines concerning options and features:

- *Non-Cancelable, Guaranteed Renewable.* This provision guarantees that the insurance company cannot terminate your policy for any reason, nor can your rates be raised. *Recommendation:* Be sure your policy contains this feature.

- *Partial Disability Benefit (also called Residual Benefit).* This provision generally pays a partial benefit if a disability prevents you from working full time. For example, if you have a heart attack and are only able to work part time, resulting in a 50 percent pay loss, your policy would pay you a 50 percent benefit. *Recommendation:* Most disabilities are less than total, so make sure your policy has this clause.

- *Waiting Period.* The waiting period is the time from the date of disability to the date when the insurance company begins making payments to you. Waiting periods are generally 90 days, 180 days, 360 days, or 730 days. Naturally, the longer the waiting period, the cheaper the premiums. *Recommendation:* Your premiums will be greatly affected by the waiting period you choose. Most people will need a 90-day waiting period until they build up sufficient cash reserves for a 180- or 360-day waiting period.

 Increasing your waiting period from 90 days to 180 days or 360 days will reduce your premiums by 10–20 percent.

- *Definition of Disability.* With life insurance, it's easy to tell if you have a claim. Disability is harder to define. You will find that the definition of disability can vary significantly from policy to policy. *Recommendation:* Find a policy that insures you in "your occupation" unless you are able to be retrained for another occupation providing a similar income.

 Avoid policies where the definition of disability is "Any Occupation" only. This means that if you are able to do anything, the insurance company will not pay.

- *Benefit Period.* The benefit period determines how long you will be paid by the insurance company. Typical choices include 2 years, 5 years, to age 65, or lifetime benefits. *Recommendation:* Statistics indicate that the average long-term disability lasts approximately 5 years. You can save a lot of money by using a 5-year benefit period rather than one that lasts until you reach age 65. However, this is not advisable unless you have a back-up income source such as your spouse's salary. Your best bet is to choose benefits payable to age 65.

- *Cost of Living Adjustments (COLA).* If you become disabled, this feature increases the benefit you will receive based on some cost-of-living index such as the Consumer Price Index (CPI). *Recommendation:* This rider is expensive. If your spouse earns a reasonable income, pass it up. If insurance will be your main source of income, consider a rider in the amount of 3–4 percent.

- *Future Insurance Option.* This feature allows you to increase your coverage periodically without having to prove you are still in good health. *Recommendation:* Buy what you need now and take the chance that as you need additional coverage you will be able to buy it later.

tip If you have a family history of serious medical illness such as diabetes or a heart condition, the Future Insurance option should be considered.

- *Social Security Rider.* Under certain conditions you are eligible to receive Social Security payments for disability. With this rider, the insurance company must pay you the Social Security benefit in the event that Social Security rejects your claim. *Recommendation:* Because Social Security rejects more than 70 percent of the claims presented, this rider is an excellent way to provide you needed coverage at a reduced cost. Buy it.

These options and features represent the core of what you want to consider as part of your disability income insurance plan. Skip other riders offered by the insurance company.

GETTING THE BEST DEAL

First, check to see if your employer provides access to group coverage. Many large employers buy this coverage for their employees. Others make it available through payroll deductions. Be sure that the group policy pays 50–70 percent of your total pay and that benefits are payable to age 65. Otherwise, you may need to supplement it with individual coverage.

If no employer group coverage is available, see if you have access to group coverage through your trade or professional organization. The premiums are usually very reasonable, but you will need to make sure that the coverage is adequate.

If no group insurance is available to you, you will need to shop the more expensive individual insurance market. Begin by deciding how much monthly income you want, how long your waiting and benefit periods will be, and what other options and features you want included.

There are many companies that write competitive disability income policies. Here are three that specialize in this type of coverage:

- *Paul Revere.* Check your yellow pages for a local agent, or call (800) 843-3426 for an agent near you.

- *Provident Life and Accident.* Check your yellow pages for a local agent, or call (800) 421-0344 for an agent near you.

- *Unum.* Check your yellow pages for a local agent, or call (800) 421-0344 for an agent near you.

For Low Load disability insurance, contact The Wholesale Insurance Network at (800) 808-5810. If you prefer working without an agent, call USAA at (800) 531-8080.

Get two or three quotes from different carriers and choose the lowest premium.

Be sure the company you choose has at least an "A" financial rating from AM Best Co., Standard & Poor's, or Moody's rating service. The company or agent can provide you with this information. The higher the rating, the better. Remember, if you suffer a truly long-term disability, you will be dependent on your insurance company to provide substantial benefits over a long period of time.

If you buy an individual disability income policy, you can cut your premiums by 15 percent if you get at least two co-workers to buy from the same company. This is called *list billing*.

Many people mistakenly think they are insured for disability because they are covered by Workers' Compensation. This state-mandated program only covers injuries sustained while on the job. It doesn't cover illness or non-job-related injuries.

Some auto loan, mortgage loan, and installment loan companies will try to sell you a disability income plan that will make your payments should you become disabled. These are overpriced policies and should be avoided unless you cannot get any disability insurance through the programs discussed in this lesson.

In this lesson, you learned how to evaluate health and disability income insurance. In the next lesson, you learn strategies for reducing your income taxes.

Smart Ways to Reduce Taxes

In this lesson, you learn simple strategies you can use to reduce your tax bill.

Tax Reduction Strategies for Everyone

If you added up all the income taxes you pay year after year, you'd undoubtedly find out the amount is extraordinarily high. While most of you can't avoid income taxes altogether, you can reduce your tax load. Whether you work for someone else or own your own company, make sure you are taking full advantage of the tax strategies available to you.

Strategy #1: Contribute to your employer-provided retirement plan. Many companies allow employees to voluntarily contribute to a retirement plan through payroll deduction. The most common type of plan is called a 401(k). In order to encourage participation, companies will often provide matching contributions. These programs create two tax advantages for you. The first is that your contribution is not subject to income taxes. For example, if you contribute $1,000, you will reduce your taxes by $200–$300. That is a 20 to 30 percent savings. The second tax advantage is that as your money grows, the interest, dividends, and gains are not subject to current income taxes. This is not true of the money you have in your personal savings account.

Strategy #2: Invest $2,000 in an Individual Retirement Account (IRA). If your employer does not have a 401(k) or other voluntary retirement plan, you and your spouse can still contribute to an Individual Retirement Account (IRA). If both you and your spouse work, you can both contribute 100 percent of your earnings, up to $2,000 each. If only one spouse works, that spouse can contribute $2,000 plus another $250 for the non-working spouse. Your IRA contribution is fully deductible if neither you nor your spouse are covered by another retirement plan. If either spouse is covered by an employer-sponsored retirement plan, your $2,000 IRA contribution may not be fully tax deductible. However, you would still benefit from tax-deferred earnings. Consult your tax advisor for details.

Strategy #3: Make your charitable contributions. As you are probably aware, your contributions to charities and religious organizations are tax deductible.

tip   If your charitable gift is for $250 or more, you must have a receipt from the charity that states the date and amount of the gift and whether you received anything in return, such as a meal. This receipt requirement only applies to single gifts for $250 or more. For example, if you send your church $200 per month, no receipt is required.

Strategy #4: Gift appreciated property. If you plan to make a donation to a charity, check to see if you have any assets, such as stock, that have a large profit due to appreciation. If you give an appreciated asset, you avoid the capital gains tax that would be due if you sold the asset personally.

If you really like the stock, buy it back with your cash. This will establish a new and higher cost basis for tax purposes. Doing so will reduce your taxes later when you sell the stock. You should not buy back the same stock within 31 days of the gift.

Strategy #5: Buy growth stocks or growth mutual funds. To avoid annual taxes on interest and dividends, invest in growth stocks instead of dividend-paying stocks or bonds and certificates of deposit.

 Growth Stocks   Growth stocks are those whose future values are derived primarily from appreciation rather than payment of dividends. (See Lesson 14 for more details.)

Strategy #6: Buy tax-free bonds. Invest in tax-free bonds and money market accounts. These types of investments are not subject to federal income taxes, and in some cases avoid state income taxes as well.

 Tax-free bonds and money market accounts should only be used if you are in the highest income tax bracket. Otherwise, you will generally be better off with a taxable bond or money market account. (See Lesson 14 for more details.)

Strategy #7: Convert non-tax-deductible interest payments to tax-deductible interest payments. If you are a homeowner, you may be eligible for a home equity line of credit. With a home equity loan, you can consolidate some or all of your other debt and the interest will then be tax deductible.

Using a home equity loan to pay off consumer debt can be hazardous to your wealth! If you can't meet your payments, you may lose your home.

Strategy #8: Offset gains with losses. If you have gains on an asset you plan to sell, see if you have other assets that have losses. This offsetting will reduce your taxes.

Strategy #9: Turn your hobby into a business. People who are self-employed have many opportunities to take deductions. If you are an artist, for example, sell your art at trade shows or local markets. You can deduct at least a portion of the cost of trips to trade shows, mileage, supplies, and so forth.

If you are self-employed or have a non-employment income such as interest, dividends, or rent, you are responsible for making quarterly estimated tax payments. It's quite easy to forget about these payments and spend your tax payment. To prevent this problem, you should calculate the taxes you will owe and save the money monthly.

If you turn your hobby into a part-time business, be sure to keep good records. To prove that your hobby is really a business, you must show a profit in three out of the past five years. Also, take only legitimate business deductions, because the chances that you'll be audited increase if you're self-employed.

tip Advance your career through education. The cost of doing so is deductible, but the benefits to you go beyond deductions. However, the cost of education to change career fields is not deductible.

Strategy #10: Buy rental real estate. Ownership of rental real estate creates a variety of deductions. One important deduction is called *depreciation*. This allows you to take a deduction for a portion of the value of the property and other assets, such as heating and air systems. You also receive a deduction for mortgage interest. These deductions usually result in a tax loss that can be used to offset a portion of your earned income.

! Rental real estate is not for amateurs. Be sure you do lots of homework before taking the plunge.

Strategy #11: Don't rent—own. There are many benefits of home ownership. One is that mortgage interest is deductible, whereas rent is not.

Along with the pride and joy of home ownership come many expenses not associated with renting. You're responsible for repairs, property taxes, and homeowners insurance. Be sure to calculate all of the costs before making the decision to buy a home. See Lesson 16, "Financial Strategies for Major Events," for more details.

tip If you have a newborn baby, be sure to apply for a Social Security number or you will not be allowed an exemption deduction.

TAX STRATEGIES FOR SELF-EMPLOYED PEOPLE

If you own your own business, you have even more opportunities to reduce your taxes. This is one of the big advantages to being self-employed. Following are some of the best tax-saving strategies available to the self-employed:

Strategy #1: Keep good records. The single biggest mistake self-employed people make is failing to keep good records. Every time you buy something, note whether it might be tax deductible. If you're unsure, save the receipt and note on the receipt the business purpose. Later, you can check with your tax advisor to determine if it is eligible.

When in doubt, deduct! In the long run, it pays to approach income tax planning aggressively.

Strategy #2: Look for deductions. Develop a tax deduction mindset. View every situation and expenditure as a possible tax deduction. For example, if you own a printing business and have a casual business lunch with a friend or acquaintance and you discuss printing personal stationery for them, you've just created a deduction under business entertainment. Don't forget business mileage, and business calls on your car phone. Count everything. With a little practice, you will be surprised at how many deductions you can create. The bonus is that your business will likely benefit as well.

tip Self-employed people can deduct 30 percent of their health insurance premiums.

Not all business expenses are immediately deductible. Some must be depreciated, which means that you deduct a portion of the expense over a certain period of time until you have fully deducted all your costs. Consult your tax advisor for details.

Strategy #3: Shift income and expenses. As you approach the end of your tax year (December for most people), complete a brief review of your tax situation. If you have had an unusually profitable year and therefore face higher taxes than normal, consider accelerating expenses and postponing income. To accelerate expenses, go ahead and purchase this year supplies or equipment that you will use early next year. To postpone income, hold off billing customers until early January of next year.

Strategy #4: Begin a Simplified Employee Pension plan (SEP). This plan allows you to contribute approximately 12 percent of your net income, up to $22,500, and receive an income tax deduction. If you have employees, they must also be included in the plan after they have worked for you during any three of the last five calendar years.

Strategy #5: Hire your children. If you can find work for them, you can pay them an income that is likely to be taxed at a much lower income tax rate than yours.

If you hire your children, no FICA or Social Security payments are required.

Use the income you pay your children to start an IRA for them. You will be amazed at what tax-deferred compound interest will do for accumulating money over a 50-year period. $1,000 invested for 50 years at 10 percent equals approximately $117,000!

In this lesson, you learned about the main strategies that can help reduce your tax bill. In the next lesson, you learn how you can accumulate more savings, whether for emergencies or retirement.

13

POWER ACCOUNTS: BUILDING FINANCIAL SELF-CONFIDENCE

In this lesson, you learn how you can build your power accounts for both short-term and long-term goals.

FINANCIAL SELF-CONFIDENCE

Your bank account balance can affect your attitude. If you're living paycheck to paycheck and an emergency happens, your finances are thrown into a tailspin. But if you have money in the bank, you're more confident that you can handle financial surprises.

This self-confidence is critical to your long-term financial success. In order to achieve and maintain this self-confidence, you need to develop both a short-term and long-term *Power Account*.

Power Account Power Accounts are investment accounts of sufficient size that you are confident you can handle any financial surprise.

First, you need a Short-Term Power Account sufficient to meet any emergencies that might arise. Next, you need a Long-Term Power Account that is consistently moving you toward your financial independence goals.

SHORT-TERM POWER ACCOUNT

You want to position yourself to deal with life's surprises. You want to have cash as a ready resource, and not have to scramble for money, or worse, borrow money to solve short-term problems.

How large should a Short-Term Power Account be? It varies, depending on your needs, but it should be large enough to give you the confidence that you can handle any financial surprise. Here are some guidelines:

- *Three Months' Take-Home Pay.* This is the minimum amount for your Short-Term Power Account. If you lose your job, this amount will allow you to meet all your regular bills and give you three months to find another job. If you are very secure in your job or feel your job skills will enable you to find another job quickly, a three-month Short-Term Power Account may be appropriate for you.

- *Six Months' Take-Home Pay.* If you are uncertain about your job security or you think that it could take a long time to find another job, you should increase your Short-Term Power Account to equal six months' take-home pay.

You may need as much as a year's net pay in your Short-Term Power Account to give you the confidence you need. Decide what the right amount is for your needs. Then begin saving toward this goal. Remember, you can never gain financial confidence without money in the bank.

STARTING YOUR SHORT-TERM POWER ACCOUNT

If you find it hard to save, you're not alone. On average, American workers save less than 3 percent of their paychecks, compared to the average Japanese workers, who save 18 percent of their paychecks. Why the difference? Perhaps the Japanese are more determined to build a sound financial future. To succeed, you must also adopt an attitude of determination. Pretend that your boss, because of economic circumstances, is forced to reduce your pay by 10 percent. Review all of your expenses to find out what you can cut in order to reduce your expenses by 10 percent. Put what you save into monthly deposits in your Short-Term Power Account.

tip   When you get your next raise, use at least half of it to increase your monthly deposits into your Power Account. The balance can then be used for living expenses.

tip   Commit at least half of any bonuses to your Power Account.

HOW TO INVEST YOUR SHORT-TERM POWER ACCOUNT

Your Short-TermPower Account should be divided between two types of investments: an interest account and mutual funds. The interest account allows you quick access to your money, while the mutual funds provide the best long-term growth.

- *Interest Account.* Start with this account and continue to fund it until it equals one month's take-home pay. If you're starting your program with less than $1,000, use a direct deposit from your paycheck to your credit union. If this isn't possible, have your bank automatically transfer your Short-Term Power Account deposit from your regular checking account to a savings account. Once you have accumulated more than $1,000, move your money to a money market fund so you can take advantage of even higher interest rates.

Money Market Fund   A money market fund is a mutual fund that invests primarily in safe, short-term investments such as certificates of deposit (CDs), commercial paper, treasuries, and banker acceptances. These funds are considered safe, and enable you to get your money any time you need it.

Contact one of the fund companies listed in Table 13.1 and ask for a new account form. Most of these funds can set up an automatic monthly withdrawal from your checking account. Also, most will allow you to write checks on your account with a $250 minimum.

Table 13.1	Good Choices for Money Market Accounts	
Money Fund and Phone Number	Minimum Initial Investment	Minimum Additional Investment
Capital Preservation (800) 472-3389	$1,000	$100
Strong Money Market (800) 368-1030	$1,000	$50
USAA Money Market (800) 382-8722	$1,000	$50

- *Mutual Funds.* The balance of your Short-Term Power Account should be invested in mutual funds (see Lesson 15 for specific details). Over the long-term, mutual funds should produce the best trade-off between returns and risks. Set up an automatic monthly withdrawal from your personal checking account to your mutual fund account.

Once you have achieved your goal for your Short-Term Power Account, you don't have to add to it. It will continue to grow through the compounding of interest. You can now shift your monthly investing to your Long-Term Power Account.

tip

If at all possible, don't ever touch your Short-Term Power Account. The purpose of the Short-Term Power Account is to build strong financial self-confidence. If you spend the money, you will "spend" your self-confidence as well. When those inevitable emergencies do arise, try to find another way to work through them. You will find that when you have money in the bank, you are mentally stronger and better at problem-solving.

Long-Term Power Account

The only way you will ever have total financial power is to be financially independent. While this process takes many years, knowing that you are systematically moving toward financial independence gives you motivation and self-confidence.

Financial Independence Financial independence is reached when your investments provide you a lifetime income sufficient to meet your lifestyle needs.

The terms financial independence and retirement are not synonymous. *Retirement* refers to that point in time when you plan to quit working. *Financial independence*, on the other hand, is that point in time when you can retire if you want to. Financial independence is about creating choice in your life.

PUTTING THE "POWER" IN YOUR LONG-TERM POWER ACCOUNT

The accumulation of money requires two elements: time and rate of return. Both are critical to achieving financial independence through your Long-Term Power Account.

THE TIME ELEMENT OF INVESTING

Giving money time to work is a key element in investing. Intuitively, you know that the sooner you start, the better off you are. What you may not know is that by starting sooner you are *much* better off.

Table 13.2 illustrates the dramatic difference in results that two investors achieved. Both earned 10 percent on their investments.

Remember, what you do now is much more important than what you do later.

Table 13.2   The Power of Investing Early

	Investor A		Investor B	
Year	Annual Investment	Ending Balance	Annual Investment	Ending Balance
1	$4,000	$4,400	$0	$0
2	4,000	9,240	0	0
3	4,000	14,564	0	0
4	4,000	20,420	0	0
5	4,000	26,862	0	0
6	4,000	33,949	0	0
7	4,000	41,744	0	0
8	4,000	50,318	0	0
9	0	55,350	4,000	4,400
10	0	60,885	4,000	9,240
11	0	66,973	4,000	14,564
12	0	73,670	4,000	20,420
13	0	81,037	4,000	26,862
14	0	89,141	4,000	33,949
15	0	98,055	4,000	41,744
16	0	107,861	4,000	50,318
17	0	118,647	4,000	59,750
18	0	130,512	4,000	70,125
19	0	143,563	4,000	81,537
20	0	157,919	4,000	94,091
21	0	173,711	4,000	107,900
22	0	191,082	4,000	123,090
23	0	210,190	4,000	139,799
24	0	231,209	4,000	158,179
25	0	254,330	4,000	178,397
26	0	279,763	4,000	200,636
27	0	307,740	4,000	225,100
28	0	338,514	4,000	252,010
29	0	372,365	4,000	281,611
30	0	409,602	4,000	314,172
31	0	450,562	4,000	349,989
32	0	495,618	4,000	389,388
33	0	545,180	4,000	432,727
34	0	599,698	4,000	480,400
35	0	659,667	4,000	532,840
36	0	725,634	4,000	590,524
37	0	798,198	4,000	653,976
38	0	878,017	4,000	723,774
39	0	965,819	4,000	800,551
40	0	1,062,401	4,000	885,006
Total	$32,000	$1,062,401	$128,000	$885,006

THE RATE OF RETURN ELEMENT OF INVESTING

The *rate of return* is the amount of money that you earn on your investment(s). It can be in the form of interest, dividends, or capital appreciation. Again, intuitively you know that the more you earn, the better. But what you may not realize is that a couple of percentage points of higher return makes a dramatic difference in your future results. Look at the two investors in the following table. By earning just two percentage points of additional return, Investor B has earned more than twice as much money over 40 years.

Table 13.3	One-Time $10,000 Investment		
	Investor A 10%	Investor B 12%	Investor B Advantage
10 years	$25,937	$31,058	+20%
20 years	$67,275	$96,422	+43%
30 years	$174,494	$299,599	+72%
40 years	$452,592	$930,509	+105%

HOW MUCH IS ENOUGH?

How much money do you need to accumulate in your Long-Term Power Account to be financially independent? Generally, you need enough money in your Power Account to produce between 60 to 100 percent of your current income for life, adjusted for future inflation.

Use Table 13.4, "Quick Start Investment Matrix," as a guide for the amount of your income you will need to invest. Just follow the steps at the bottom of the table.

Table 13.4

Quick Start
Investment Matrix

	Target Earnings Rate							
	7%	8%	9%	10%	11%	12%	13%	14%
Years until Retirement								
20	50%	40%	33%	28%	24%	20%	19%	16%
25	35%	28%	23%	20%	16%	13%	12%	9%
30	27%	20%	16%	13%	10%	9%	7%	6%
35	21%	15%	12%	9%	7%	5%	4%	3.5%
40	17%	11%	9%	6%	5%	4%	2.5%	2%

Step 1. Choose the number of years until financial independence target age.
Step 2. Choose your Target Earnings Rate.
Step 3. The point at which Step 1 and Step 2 intersect is the percent of your gross income that must be invested.

The key to the Quick Start Program is that as your income rises, the percentage of your income that you invest does not change. The amount of money you invest increases with each pay raise.

This program gets you started for now, but eventually you want to make more precise calculations. To help you, get a free retirement planning kit available from T. Rowe Price at (800) 638-5660. Computer buffs might want to use Quicken, which is available at any computer store. Also, Fidelity Investments offers an excellent software program for less than $20.

If you are not investing at least 10 percent of your gross pay, you are not on the road to financial independence!

In this lesson, you learned the power of Power Accounts. In the next lesson, you learn the advantages and disadvantages of various investment options available to you.

· 14 ·

UNDERSTANDING YOUR INVESTMENT CHOICES

In this lesson, you learn about the various investment choices you have as well as how to choose the right investments to meet your needs.

MAKING SOUND INVESTMENT CHOICES

There are literally thousands of choices you can make when deciding how to invest your money. However, investing need not be an impossible task. Once you understand the basic characteristics of each type of investment, you will be ready to begin developing your investment strategy.

What follows is a rundown of the many types of investments, from the more familiar bank accounts to the riskier investments that are appropriate for only a few of you.

CHECKING ACCOUNTS

Checking accounts are transaction accounts that pay no interest or very low interest. Basic fees are charged either monthly or on a per-transaction basis.

Recommendation: You should use checking accounts to pay your monthly bills rather than as a place to store large amounts of cash.

Because you don't want to keep large amounts of cash in your checking account, look for an account with low fees rather than a high interest rate.

BANK SAVINGS ACCOUNTS

Most banks allow you to open a savings account with a deposit of as little as $25. Fees for maintaining the account are nominal or nonexistent, and the interest you earn is very low, typically 2–4 percent. You can withdraw your money anytime.

Recommendation: If you are just starting your investment program and don't have a lot of money, a bank savings account is a good choice.

To force the savings habit, have your bank automatically transfer money from your checking account to your savings account each month. To do so, both accounts must be at the same bank.

CREDIT UNIONS

Many industries have developed their own banking institutions, called *credit unions*, to serve their members. Credit unions operate much like banks in that they offer savings accounts, make loans, and so forth. Typically, you can withdraw your money at any time. However, credit unions are not legal banks and are, therefore, not subject to the same level of regulation. The result is that their overhead is low and they generally offer higher interest rates on savings accounts. Credit unions are not insured by the Federal Deposit Insurance Corporation. Make certain your credit union is financially sound.

Recommendation: If you are a member of a credit union, but don't have a lot of money now, this is your best bet.

 tip To encourage the savings habit, have your employer make payroll deductions to your credit union.

MONEY MARKET FUNDS AND ACCOUNTS

Money market funds are offered through mutual fund companies, and money market accounts are offered through banks. Most require a minimum initial investment of $1,000, but charge no fees. You are able to withdraw your money at any time. The interest paid on these accounts is generally the highest of the options already mentioned.

Recommendation: Once you have built up enough money in your savings or credit union account to open a money market fund, you should do so. Use this account to hold one month's net pay as described in your Short-Term Power Account plan (see Lesson 13, "Power Accounts: Building Financial Self-Confidence").

CERTIFICATES OF DEPOSIT (CDs)

CDs are offered primarily by banks. You agree to leave your money with the bank for a fixed period of time, such as three months, six months, two years, and so on. You're paid a fixed interest rate until the CD matures. Because you agree not to withdraw your money for a stated period of time, you generally receive a higher interest rate on a CD than on other types of bank accounts. You'll be subject to stiff penalties if you withdraw your money prior to maturity.

Recommendation: If you think you'll need your money in a relatively short period of time—less than five years—or you are a very conservative investor, CDs may be a good choice for you.

FIXED ANNUITIES

Fixed annuities are sold by insurance companies. They are similar to CDs in that they offer a fixed interest rate, usually for one year. They have an added advantage: the interest earnings are not subject to current income taxes. At retirement, you can convert your annuity into a lifetime income and receive a fixed annual income for as long as you live. However, you no longer have access to your principle.

The disadvantage of annuities is that they carry hefty expenses, and often commissions as well. Also, if you cash in your annuity before you reach age 59 1/2, the federal government imposes a 10-percent penalty in addition to the income taxes you owe. Most insurance companies also impose penalties if you cash in your policy during the first 5–10 years.

Recommendation: Fixed annuities are rarely a good choice for your short- or long-term investment strategy.

WHOLE LIFE AND UNIVERSAL LIFE INSURANCE

These policies contain a life insurance element and an investment or savings element. With whole life insurance, your savings account is credited with yearly dividends from the insurance company. Dividend rates are typically modest and somewhat comparable to long-term CDs. With universal life policies, your savings account is credited with interest based on prevailing rates and is comparable to rates paid by longer-term CDs. The interest rates on universal life policies fluctuate more than the dividends on whole life policies.

Recommendation: Generally, you shouldn't buy whole life and universal life insurance policies as part of your investment strategy. For more information on these products, see Lesson 7, "Understanding Life Insurance."

BONDS

Bonds are debt investments issued by the federal government (treasury bonds), municipalities (municipal bonds), corporations (corporate bonds), and mortgage holders (Government National Mortgage Association, GNMA). The terms of each include the interest rate, how often interest is paid, when the bond matures, and the face amount of the bond. In effect, you are lending money to the institution that issues the bond, and the institution is agreeing to pay you interest until you get your money back.

 Bond Maturity   The bond maturity refers to the date that you get your money back. *Face Amount* refers to how much money you get back at maturity.

Maturities range from a few weeks or months to 20 years or more. The longer the maturity, the higher the interest rate you will receive. Also, the longer the maturity, the greater your risk. That's because the longer the maturity, the greater the risk that you won't get your principle back because the bond issuer could go bankrupt. Also, the longer the maturity, the more likely general interest rates will rise above the rate you are currently being paid. This causes your bond to be worth less if you try to sell it before it matures.

The quality of a bond varies according to the financial strength of the issuer. Lower quality bonds carry an increased risk of default and, therefore, must offer investors a higher interest rate to entice them to invest. The safest bonds are Treasury bonds issued by the federal government.

Many bonds are rated by independent rating services such as Standard & Poor's and Moody's. The rating scale typically runs from AAA, the highest, to B, the lowest.

tip A bond that is not rated may not be a high-risk investment. Bond issuers must pay to have their bonds rated. Some choose not to and pass the savings on to you in the form of higher interest rates.

You can either purchase individual bonds or you can invest in a bond mutual fund.

Recommendation: If you are a conservative to moderate risk investor, bonds will be an important part of your portfolio. However, unless you have a thorough knowledge of the bond market, your best choice is to invest in a bond mutual fund. For more information on investing in bond mutual funds, see Lesson 15, "Developing Your Investment Strategy."

STOCKS

When you buy a stock, you are buying ownership in a corporation. If the company does well, you do well. If it does poorly, you do poorly. If it goes bankrupt, you lose your money. In essence, your money is tied to the company's fate. It can be exciting and rewarding, but also risky. You can buy either individual stocks or stock mutual funds.

Recommendation: Stocks should be an important part of your investment strategy. For a variety of reasons that will be discussed later, you should invest in stock mutual funds rather than attempt to buy individual stocks. See Lesson 15 for more details.

VARIABLE ANNUITIES

Variable annuities, like the fixed annuities mentioned earlier in this lesson, are sold by insurance companies. They have all of the characteristics of fixed annuities, with two exceptions. First, rather than receiving a fixed interest rate, you select from a variety of mutual funds. Typical choices include a money market fund, a bond fund, a stock fund, and, in some cases, an international stock fund. The second difference is that variable annuities expenses are even higher than those of fixed annuities.

Recommendation: The main advantage of the variable annuity is the tax deferral of gains. Because of relatively high expenses and limited choice of funds, you should generally avoid this product. If you are interested in variable annuities, consider no-load companies such as Vanguard (800-522-5555), Scudder (800-225-2470), and Charles Schwab & Co. (800-838-0650).

 No-Load   No-load means that the product is sold without a sales charge. You deal directly with the company, not a salesperson.

VARIABLE LIFE INSURANCE

Variable life insuranceis similar to the variable annuity, with two exceptions. First, there is life insurance in addition to your investment account. Second, the expenses are even higher than the expenses in the variable annuity. It does have one distinct advantage over the variable annuity, however. If you hold your variable life policy until you die, the profits from your investment account and the life insurance itself escape income taxes. This is not true with the variable annuity.

Recommendation: You may find the concept that a variable life policy performs "double duty" as both life insurance and long-term investment appealing. But, due to high expenses and limited mutual fund options, a better choice is to buy a competitive level term policy and invest your money using no-load mutual funds. For more information on life insurance, see Lesson 7, "Understanding Life Insurance."

INTERNATIONAL SECURITIES

International securities include both foreign stocks and bonds. In addition to the normal risks associated with stocks and bonds, you are also subject to the risks of currency fluctuations.

Currency Risk   Currency risk refers to the risk that a stock or bond will fluctuate in value due to the change in value of the foreign currency relative to the U.S. dollar.

Recommendation: International securities represent over 60 percent of the securities marketplace. They will be an important part of your investment strategy. Your best choice is international mutual funds. See Lesson 15, "Developing Your Investment Strategy," for more details on how to use international mutual funds in your investment program.

MUTUAL FUNDS

A mutual fund is a company that hires professional investment managers to buy stocks and bonds. The typical fund will own 50 or more individual securities. When you give them your money, you own shares of each security in the fund. These funds provide liquidity, and you can receive your account values within a few days. Many mutual funds concentrate their assets in a particular type of security, such as large company stocks, short-term government bonds, and so on. This allows you to build a "tailored" portfolio.

Recommendation: For reasons explained in Lesson 15, mutual funds are the best choice for your investment strategy.

EXOTIC INVESTMENTS

More exotic investments include partnerships, options and futures contracts, and collectibles. Each of these should be avoided by all but the most experienced investors. Investment real estate and precious metals should only be purchased through a mutual fund where you have professional management.

In this lesson, you learned about your various investment options. In the next lesson, you learn how to develop an investment strategy tailored to your needs.

15

DEVELOPING YOUR INVESTMENT STRATEGY

In this lesson, you learn how to develop your own investment strategy using mutual funds.

WHY MUTUAL FUNDS?

Of all available investment options, mutual funds are the best choice for two reasons:

- *Professional Management.* When you invest in a mutual fund, you are in effect turning your money over to a full-time professional money manager and team of investment analysts. These people work full-time at analyzing and investing in companies on your behalf. Because you have pooled your money with hundreds or even thousands of other investors, the fee you pay for these professional management services is a modest 1/2–2 percent (called *operating expenses*) per year.

- *Diversification.* The second advantage of investing in a mutual fund is that you get instant diversification. This is because most mutual funds own 50 or more individual securities. By investing $1,000, you own your proportionate share of each security in the fund. This would be impossible to do if you tried to buy the individual securities, because your trading costs (commissions) would be prohibitive.

Diversification significantly reduces the risk of a portfolio. For example, if a stock your mutual fund owns becomes worthless, it has very little impact on the portfolio as a whole because the other 49 stocks may be doing well.

Diversification   Diversification is the process of reducing portfolio risk by spreading your investment dollars over a significantly large number of securities.

Investment Choices in Mutual Funds

Mutual funds can be divided into three broad groups: stock funds, bond funds, and money market funds. Each group can then be subdivided into many subgroups. For example, under stock funds you have large company stock funds, small company stock funds, international stock funds, sector stock funds, value stock funds—the list goes on and on. The same is true for bond and money market funds. You can now choose from more than 7,000 funds.

You can easily tailor an investment portfolio to your specific needs using mutual funds. And you have the advantage of professional management, low costs, and diversification.

Load versus No-Load Funds

With mutual funds, you can buy either a *load fund,* in which a sales commission is paid, or a *no-load fund,* which means no sales commission is paid.

Some load funds charge a front-end commission that typically ranges from 5–6 percent. Other funds hide the commission in the form of a back-end load, in which you are charged a commission if you leave the fund within the first few years, usually within 5 years. Either way, you are paying a large commission to a salesperson. Paying sales commission is a waste of money and should be avoided. There is no empirical evidence to suggest that investors are better off buying a load fund over a no-load fund.

Some load fund salespeople claim that load funds are cheaper than no-load funds in the long run because load funds charge smaller annual management fees. This is not the case. While there are always exceptions, you need look no further than the Vanguard family of no-load funds to find the lowest annual management fees in the industry.

Understanding the Risk/Return Relationship

If your money is properly invested, the greater the risks you take, the greater the returns you can expect over time, and vice versa. For example, certificates of deposit (CDs) carry very little risk and therefore pay very modest returns. Stocks carry much higher risks but (historically speaking) have produced much higher returns.

As you develop your investment strategy, you must find the balance of risks you are willing to assume and the returns you need to earn to meet your objectives. You can call your local bank to get an idea of what CDs and other so-called "safe" investments are earning. For historical returns on stocks and bonds, see the following table.

Historical Returns for Different Investments
Annualized Returns for Periods Ended 9/30/95

	50 Years	20 Years	10 Years	5 Years
Large Company Stocks	13.8%	16.9%	17.2%	13.2%
Small Company Stocks	17.4%	23.1%	14.5%	16.4%
Foreign Stocks	N/A	18.3%	20.9%	5.2%
Intermediate-Term U.S. Government Bonds	5.9%	9.9%	10.6%	9.1%
Treasury Bills	4.7%	7.3%	5.8%	4.9%
Real Estate	N/A	14.11%	8.01%	2.78%
Precious Metals	N/A	7.74%	1.71%	1.14%
U.S. Inflation	4.4%	5.4%	3.5%	3.4%

tip It is very difficult, if not impossible, to achieve financial independence by investing in CDs and other "safe" investments alone. This is because of the long-term effect inflation has on the purchasing power (value) of your money.

tip When investing in stocks, you will encounter fluctuating values and sometimes losses. In a properly diversified portfolio, the problem of volatility is solved over time, typically three to five years. This means that stock market values go up more than they go down over time.

THE IMPORTANCE OF ASSET ALLOCATION

Asset allocation means that you divide your money among different *types* of investments, called asset classes. Examples are large company stocks, small company stocks, U.S. bonds, and international bonds.

The use of asset allocation in your portfolio reduces the risks because the different asset classes react differently to a given set of economic or financial circumstances. For example, during a period of rising U.S. inflation, domestic stocks may do poorly, but precious metals, real estate, and international stocks may do well. The result of having multiple asset classes in your portfolio should be reduced volatility.

 Studies indicate that your asset allocation decisions are even more important than your investment selection decisions.

DESIGNING YOUR PORTFOLIO

To aid you in designing your portfolio, use the three-step process that follows.

STEP 1: MAKE YOUR ASSET ALLOCATION DECISIONS

In making your asset allocation decisions, you are deciding the appropriate mix of stocks, bonds, and money markets based on your risk tolerance and return objectives. Obviously, you would like very high returns with no risk, but unfortunately, that's not the way the market works.

Using the following table, choose a portfolio that best matches your risk/return profile. Portfolios are numbered 1 through 5. Number 1 is the least risky and number 5 is the most risky. Below each portfolio is the recommended asset class allocation.

	Low Risk Low Return ←			→ High Risk High Return	
	#1	#2	#3	#4	#5
1-Year Down Side Risks (2)	-.5%	-4.5%	-7%	-11%	-16%
Target Annualized 5-Year Returns (2)	8-9%	10-11%	12-13%	14-15%	15%+
ASSET CLASSES					
U.S. Large Company	15%	25%	12%	20%	15%
U.S. Small/Mid Size Company	0%	10%	20%	30%	60%
International Stocks	5%	10%	15%	20%	25%
Intermediate Bonds	45%	40%	45%	20%	0%
Short-Term Bonds	35%	10%	0%	0%	0%
Real Estate	0%	5%	8%	10%	0%
Precious Metals (3)	0%	0%	0%	0%	0%
Money Markets (1)	0%	0%	0%	0%	0%
	100%	100%	100%	100%	100%

(1) Assumes you have your Short-Term Power Account in place (Lesson 13) so no money market investments are needed in your portfolio.
(2) No investment results can ever be guaranteed. Risks and returns are targets only, not guarantees. Statistics are based on 90% confidence levels and historical data from 1/1/75 through 12/31/95 and 1/1/85 through 12/31/95.
(3) Precious metals are a hedge (insurance position) and should represent 0-10% of your portfolio.

STEP 2: MAKE YOUR FUND SELECTION

Once you have chosen the appropriate portfolio for you, use the following tables to select the appropriate funds to fill each asset class in your portfolio. To make the selection easier, the funds are divided into their appropriate asset class. (Statistical data based on year-end 1995.)

Asset Class	Fund Name + Phone Number	Operating Expense	Minimum Initial Purchase - Personal/ IRA	Subsequent Purchases - Personal/ IRA	Annualized Return -			Worst Year	Best Year
					3-Year	5-Year	10-Year		
U.S. Large Company	Vanguard US Growth (800-662-7447)	0.44%	$3000 / $500	$3000 / $500	12.33	16.41	12.99	'87* -6.07	'95* +38.44
U.S. Large Company	20th Century Ultra Investors (800-345-2021)	1.00%	$2500 / $0	$50 / $0	17.36	25.00	19.81	'84 -19.45	'91 +86.45
U.S. Large Company	Fidelity Value (800-544-8888)	1.08%	$2500 / $500	$2500 / $500	18.93	20.79	14.07	'90 -12.82	'82 +35.17
U.S. Large Company	Schwab 1000 (800-526-8600)	0.54%	$1000 / $500	$1000 / $500	14.37	-	-	N/A	N/A
U.S. Large Company	Vanguard Index 500 (800-662-7447)	0.19%	$3000 / $500	$3000 / $500	15.18	16.41	14.58	'77 -7.84	'95 +37.45
U.S. Medium Company	Mutual Beacon (800-553-3014)	0.75%	$5000 / $200	$5000 / $200	17.79	18.76	15.64	'90* -8.17	'80* +30.38
U.S. Medium Company	Nicholas (414-272-6133)	0.77%	$500 / $500	$50 / $500	11.68	17.37	13.20	'90* -4.81	'91* +41.98
U.S. Medium Company	Nicholas II (414-272-6133)	0.66%	$1000 / $1000	$1000 / $1000	11.38	16.10	12.50	'90 -6.28	'91 +39.56
U.S. Medium Company	SteinRow Special (800-338-2550)	1.02%	$2500 / $500	$1000 / $500	11.38	16.13	14.71	'81* -11.19	'80* +51.05
U.S. Small Company	Fidelity Low-Priced Stock (800-544-8888)	1.11%	$2500 / $500	$2500 / $500	16.31	24.30	-	'90 -0.08	'91 +46.26
U.S. Small Company	Schwab Small Cap Index (800-526-8600)	0.68%	$1000 / $500	$1000 / $500	-	-	-	N/A	N/A
U.S. Small Company	Vanguard Index Small Cap Stock (800-662-7447)	0.17%	$3000 / $500	$3000 / $500	14.99	21.16	10.62	'84* -25.17	'82 +45.97

Asset Class	Fund Name + Phone Number	Operating Expense	Minimum Initial Purchase - Personal/ IRA	Subsequent Purchases - Personal/ IRA	Annualized Return -			Worst Year	Best Year
					3-Year	5-Year	10-Year		
International Stock	Fidelity Overseas (800-544-8888)	1.24%	$2500 / $500	$2500 / $500	15.65	8.27	13.42	'92 -11.46	'85 +78.67
International Stock	Schwab International Index (800-526-8600)	0.85%	$1000 / $500	$1000 / $500	-	-	-	N/A	N/A
International Stock	Scudder International (800-225-2470)	1.19%	$1000 / $500	$50 / $500	14.11	10.09	12.94	'90* -8.92	'86* +50.69
International Stock	T. Rowe Price International Stock (800-638-5660)	0.96%	$2500 / $1000	$50 / $1000	15.70	11.62	14.90	'90 -8.89	'86 +61.29
International Stock	Vanguard International Growth (800-662-7447)	0.58%	$3000 / $500	$3000 / $500	18.77	10.58	13.57	'90 -12.05	'85 +56.95
Bonds	Fidelity Intermediate Bond (800-544-8888)	0.68%	$2500 / $500	$2500 / $500	7.37	8.49	8.38	'94* -2.01	'82* +24.96
Bonds	T. Rowe Price New Income (800-638-5660)	0.78%	$2500 / $1000	$50 / $1000	8.08	8.89	8.85	'94* -2.21	'82* +24.12
Bonds	Vanguard Bond Index Fund Intermediate-Term (800-662-7747)	0.18%	$3000 / $500	$3000 / $500	-	-	-	N/A	N/A
Bonds	Vanguard Fixed-Income GNMA (800-662-7447)	0.30%	$3000 / $500	$3000 / $500	7.06	8.90	9.18	'94 -0.95	'82 +31.56
Short-Term Bonds	Fidelity Short-Term Bond (800-544-8888)	0.69%	$2500 / $500	$2500 / $500	4.75	7.07	-	'94 -4.09	'91 +14.03

Asset Class	Fund Name + Phone Number	Operating Expense	Minimum Initial Purchase - Personal/ IRA	Subsequent Purchases - Personal/ IRA	Annualized Return -			Worst Year	Best Year
					3-Year	5-Year	10-Year		
Short-Term Bonds	Scudder Short-Term Bond (800-225-2470)	0.73%	$1000 / $500	$50 / $500	5.07	6.94	7.95	'94 -2.87	'85 +20.91
Short-Term Bonds	Vanguard Fixed-Income Short-Term Corporate (800-662-7447)	0.28%	$3000 / $500	$3000 / $500	6.43	7.88	8.27	'94 -0.08	'85 +14.90
Short-Term Bonds	Vanguard Bond Index Short-Term (800-662-7447)	0.18%	$3000 / $500	$3000 / $500	-	-	-	N/A	N/A
Real Estate	Cohen & Steers (800-437-9912)	1.14%	$10000**		12.64	-	-	N/A	N/A
Real Estate	Fidelity Real Estate Investment (800-544-8888)	1.03%	$2500 / $500	$2500 / $500	8.39	16.20	-	'90 -8.70	'91 +39.19
Precious Metals	Invesco Strategic Gold (800-525-8085)	1.07%	$1000 / $250	$50 / $250	11.97	3.64	3.69	'94 -27.85	'93 +72.63
Precious Metals	Lexington Goldfund (800-526-0056)	1.54%	$1000 / $250	$500 / $250	19.36	4.88	7.53	'81 -32.24	'93 +86.96
Precious Metals	Vanguard Specialized Gold & Precious Metals (800-662-7447)	0.25%	$3000 / $500	$3000 / $500	20.43	8.00	10.60	'90 -19.86	'93 +93.36

tip   If you are just starting your investment program and do not have enough money to invest in each of the various asset classes, start your program by buying a U.S. Large Company stock fund. Continue to save until you have enough money to buy a bond fund. Continue this process until you have positions in all asset classes.

tip   If you want to own the funds of several different fund companies, use a discount broker such as Charles Schwab & Co. (800 526-8600).

In this lesson, you learned how to develop and implement an investment strategy tailored to your needs. In the next lesson, you learn how to plan for major events such as buying a home or starting a family.

16

Financial Strategies for Major Events

In this lesson, you learn how to develop plans for dealing with the major events in your life.

Dealing with Life's Major Events

You'll have to deal with a variety of significant life events. By examining two typical major events, you learn the skill of strategic planning. These two major events are the birth of a child and the buying and financing of a home.

Financial Strategies When Expecting a Child

Few events bring you into financial focus as quickly as the realization that you will soon have a baby. You'll spend an added $5,000 to $7,000 during your child's first year. By the time your child is 18, you should expect to have spent another

$100,000 to $250,000. Then there's college. Add another $100,000 to $250,000. Having children represents a major financial commitment. The following checklist will help you keep your finances on track:

- *Raise your cash reserves to at least $5,000.* This will give you breathing room in case of an emergency.

- *Check your health insurance policy.* Hospital and physician charges for delivering a baby range from $6,000 to $10,000 or more. Find out what portion your medical insurance will pay and then begin saving for the balance using a money market account.

- *Review your life insurance.* If this is your first child, your life insurance needs are likely to increase significantly (see Lesson 8, "How Much Life Insurance Is Enough?").

- *Review your disability income insurance.* Make sure your disability income insurance would replace 60–70 percent of your income (see Lesson 11, "Health and Disability Income Insurance").

- *Draw up a will.* If you already have a will, review it. It will likely need to be updated. Your will should name a *guardian*, a person who is responsible for your child's day-to-day upbringing. Choose someone with similar values to your own. Your will should also establish a trust and trustees for managing your assets for the benefit of your children.

If you don't appoint a guardian, one will be appointed by a judge, who won't know your family or your wishes.

- *Rework your budget.* Develop a revised budget that includes your expected changes in income and expenses during the six months prior to your child's birth and the twelve months afterward. A good rule of thumb is to increase your expenses by $300 to $500 per month. Also, if one spouse plans to take an unpaid leave of absence from work, you need to further adjust your budget and, if you plan to use day care, check the costs in your area.

- *Begin saving for college.* The cost of college is enormous. The sooner you start the easier it will be. Begin with $50 per month and increase the amount you are saving each time you get a raise. Remember, you'll need between $100,000 and $250,000 to cover each child's future college costs.

 tip   For help in college planning, read the *10 Minute Guide to Getting into College* by O'Neal Turner.

Having children requires sacrifices. Plan in advance to minimize the financial surprises and the stress.

FINANCIAL STRATEGIES WHEN BUYING A HOME

Buying a home is likely to be the single largest investment you ever make. For most people, it requires borrowing large sums of money.

When buying a home, you must answer four major questions: 1) How much should I spend on a home? 2) How much down payment do I need? 3) What is the best type of mortgage for me? 4) Should I buy a 15- or 30-year mortgage? The following sections will help you answer these important questions.

HOW MUCH SHOULD I SPEND ON A HOME?

One of the biggest and most common financial mistakes is to over-extend yourself when you buy a home. The result may be financial stress when you find that you have little or no money left over after paying the mortgage for savings, gifts, or vacations.

To keep your finances on track, use the following Home Buyers Worksheet as a guide for how much to spend on your home. Also review Lesson 5, "Guidelines for Borrowing," for additional guidelines.

HOME BUYERS WORKSHEET

STEP 1   Example

Enter your total annual income here.   60,000
Example: Total annual income is $60,000.

STEP 2

From Table 16.1, locate the factor for either a 30-year mortgage or a 15-year mortgage that corresponds to current mortgage interest rates.

Enter the factor here.   2.20
Example: Current interest rates on a 30-year mortgage = 7%. From the following table, locate the factor for a 30-year mortgage at 7% = 2.20.

continues

HOME BUYERS WORKSHEET

STEP 3

Multiply your answer in Step 1 by your
answer in Step 2 and enter here.   132,000
Example: 60,000 × 2.20 = $132,000.

STEP 4

Enter the amount of money available for
your down payment here.   12,000
Example: You've saved $12,000 toward your
down payment.

STEP 5

Add your answer from Step 3 to your answer
in Step 4.   144,000
Example: $132,000 + $12,000 = $144,000.

THIS IS THE MOST YOU SHOULD SPEND
ON YOUR HOME.

TABLE 16.1   MORTGAGE FACTORS

CURRENT MORTGAGE INTEREST RATES	30-YEAR MORTGAGE FACTOR	15-YEAR MORTGAGE FACTOR
4%	3.10	2.00
5%	2.80	1.90
6%	2.50	1.80
7%	2.20	1.65
8%	2.00	1.60

CURRENT MORTGAGE INTEREST RATES	30-YEAR MORTGAGE FACTOR	15-YEAR MORTGAGE FACTOR
9%	1.85	1.45
10%	1.70	1.40
11%	1.50	1.30
12%	1.40	1.25

HOW MUCH DOWN PAYMENT DO I NEED?

The idealx down payment is 20 percent of the total price of your home. By putting down 20 percent, you avoid Private Mortgage Insurance (PMI). PMI is a monthly fee charged by mortgage companies to borrowers whose down payment is less than 20 percent. Paying PMI can increase your effective interest rate by 1/4 percent or more.

WHAT IS THE BEST TYPE OF MORTGAGE FOR ME?

The two types of mortgages you should consider are *fixed rate mortgages* and *adjustable rate mortgages* (ARM). With the fixed rate mortgage, your interest rate and payments remain the same throughout the life of your loan. With an ARM, both your interest rate and payments are subject to change each year. Your interest rate will change based on changes in some nationally recognized interest rate such as the one-year Treasury Bill rate. The first-year interest rate for an ARM mortgage is typically less than the rate for a fixed-rate mortgage. This difference can be 1 to 2 percent or more.

The first-year interest rate on an ARM loan is a subsidized rate. Even if general interest rates do not change, your interest rate and mortgage payments will rise at your next anniversary. When comparing ARM rates to fixed rates, be sure to ask the lender what the nonsubsidized ARM rate would be. Also, be sure your ARM loan has an annual and lifetime interest rate cap. The interest rate on most loans cannot increase more than 2 percent per year or 6 percent lifetime.

If you plan to keep your house for less than five years, consider the ARM loan. You will benefit from the lower payments in the early years. Make certain you calculate how high your payments could be when your ARM is adjusted. You need to be comfortable that your budget will be able to handle the increases.

If you plan to keep your home more than five years, consider a fixed rate mortgage. You will benefit from the security of a fixed payment.

SHOULD I BUY A 15- OR 30-YEAR MORTGAGE?

There are two advantages to a 15-year mortgage. First, you build up equity faster. Second, these mortgages typically carry a lower interest rate. This is because the lender is getting its money back faster, which reduces the risk of the loan. If your cash flow permits, use a 15-year mortgage rather than a 30-year.

If you want help finding low mortgage rates, contact HSH Associates at **(800) 873-2837**. For a small fee, they will provide you with a list of competitive lenders in your area, as well as details of the various loan programs they offer. Also, Mortgage Market Information Services at **(800) 509-4636** surveys 300 newspapers from around the country. They will fax you a summary at no cost.

Consider refinancing your existing mortgage if current mortgage rates are 1 1/2 percent to 2 percent below your current rate *and* you plan to keep your present home for at least five more years.

In this lesson, you learned the best ways to deal with some major life events.

This book provides you with the basic information you need to build a sound financial future together. As your financial situation becomes more complex, you may find that you need help from a professional advisor. The Institute of Certified Financial Planners (ICFP) will provide you two or three names of professionals in your area. If you prefer to deal with someone who does not sell products, ask for fee-only advisors. Call 1-800-282-7526.

INDEX